The Prince

ST MARTIN'S PRESS   NEW YORK

Machiavelli's

THE PRINCE

A Bilingual Edition

TRANSLATED AND EDITED BY

Mark Musa, INDIANA UNIVERSITY

Introduction

It is ironic that a man as devoted to the service of his state and country as Niccolò Machiavelli should have his name used to represent everything he was not. To be "Machiavellian" is to be treacherous, double-dealing, crafty, and cruel; Machiavelli himself was none of these. Born into a noble family in Florence on May 3, 1469, he grew up during the turbulent reign of Lorenzo de' Medici. The Italy of Machiavelli's youth was torn apart by internal strife and war. The most important Italian states—Milan, Venice, the Papal States, Naples, Florence, and Genoa—were constantly plotting and quarreling with France and Spain and with each other, anxious to enlarge their territories and increase their strength. Between 1494 and 1496 five different kings had reigned in Naples.

Machiavelli received his first influential position with the government of Florence in 1498, a month after Savonarola was hanged, then burned, on the gibbet in the great square. He was appointed Chancellor and Secretary to the *Dieci di Libertà e Pace*, a post he held until the fall of the republican regime in 1512. His position allowed him to travel: he was often sent on legations to neighboring states and other countries (twice to the Court of Rome and four times to the Court of France), and during his travels he observed how various princes and other countries managed their affairs. Certainly his embassy to Cesare Borgia during the revolt of Arezzo was significant. He spent October 1502 to January 1503 at the court of the Borgias, and, while Chapter vii of *The Prince* reveals Machiavelli's admiration for Borgia, it also indicates that

these were three months of dispassionate examination of how this memorable figure adroitly governed his state.

His post also gave him the opportunity to study military matters. While Florence was at war with Pisa he realized the harmfulness of mercenaries, which he saw as a chief cause of Italy's economic and political chaos—a theme of major importance in *The Prince*. Machiavelli argued so convincingly against mercenary troops that he finally persuaded the government of Florence to form a citizen army in 1506. In 1507 he was appointed Chancellor of the *Nove della Milizia*, the governing body of the militia.

In September 1512 the Florentine Republic came to an end; Piero Soderini, its head, was deposed and banished by a Spanish papal army, and the Medici returned to rule once more. In November Machiavelli was relieved of all his duties and his post given to Niccolò Michelozzi. His fortunes continued to decline: the following year his name was found on a list of alleged conspirators against the Medici and he was imprisoned. After his release several months later through the intervention of the new Medici Pope, Leo X, he retired to his country farm near Florence with his wife and four children. Here he remained, without stipend, for twelve years, now in the service of literature.

In 1513 Machiavelli began *The Prince*, which he probably completed by the end of the year, and the *Discourses on the First Ten Books of Titus Livy*. After completing the *Discourses* in 1517, and while composing the *Art of War*, published in seven books in 1521, Machiavelli sought, in a modest way, to return to public life. During these years several powerful Medici died; with the passing of Guiliano in 1516, then Lorenzo and his wife in 1519, control of Florentine affairs fell to the hands of the Medici Cardinal, Giulio, who asked Machiavelli, among others, for his suggestions for a new constitution. Machia-

velli gave these in his *Discourse on the Reform of the Government of Florence* in 1519. In 1520 the Signoria of Florence sent him to Lucca to settle some business affairs, and during his stay there he wrote the amusing *Life of Castruccio Castracani*. Later in the same year, at the request of Cardinal Guilio de' Medici, the Studio of Florence commissioned him to write the *History of Florence*.

To think of Machiavelli as only a political-historical writer would be wrong, for he was also a leading dramatist of his age; indeed, *Mandragola*, written around 1518, is considered one of the best plays ever written in any language. In his purely literary works, particularly the plays *Andria*, *Mandragola*, and *Clizia*, Machiavelli exercises his command of the language, his sense of the dramatic in everyday life, and his understanding of the instincts that cause men to act—elements all present to some degree in *The Prince*.

Machiavelli's literary works—including his unfinished poem in *terza rima*, *The Golden Ass*, his entertaining short story *Belfagor*, and the *Dialogue on Language*—are better appreciated if they are not treated as directories of examples and key phrases that explicate *The Prince* or the *Discourses*; they are works of art in their own right. All of Machiavelli's writings, however, share a common vision: man is the center of his focus—not man in relation to his creator, but rather in relation to his secular environment. Though Machiavelli never denies the existence of God, and occasionally pays Him lip-service, he does push Him out of the clear focus He enjoyed during the Middle Ages. Mysticism has given way to realism, God to man, the Middle Ages to the Renaissance. In his literary works, as in *The Prince*, Machiavelli is concerned with "things as they really are" and not "things as they ought to be"—the *verità effettuale*, the "effectual truth."

The best introduction to the man and his writings, and

crucial to understanding Machiavelli's thought, are his many letters. They show his preoccupation with the political scene as well as his personal problems. Ideas developed later in *The Prince* are scattered throughout these letters, which, above all, reveal the author of *The Prince* as an honest and loyal servant of his state and country, respectful before ingenuity (*virtù*) and humble before fortune (*fortuna*). Niccolò Machiavelli witnessed the return of his Florence to a republican form of government in 1527. He died on June 22 of the same year.

Paradoxically, the success of *The Prince* comes largely from the fact that it has been misunderstood. Many critics have failed to recognize that the age he lived in and the conditions of his country determined much of Machiavelli's doctrine. No one need marvel at Chapter XVIII: "How a Prince Should Keep His Word," for in 1513 no state kept promises that did not suit it. The muscular, colorful style of *The Prince* makes it easy to isolate sentences and phrases, and these epigrams, taken out of context, have further contributed to *The Prince's* malodorous history. And because many readers did not see, or would not accept, the focus of the writer, they burdened the text and the author with their own attitudes and feelings.

In Chapter xv of *The Prince*, Machiavelli makes his intentions clear, for he is well aware that he is doing something new, that he is dealing with his material in a new way:

But, my intention being to write something useful . . . it seemed to me more appropriate to pursue the effectual truth (*la verità effettuale*) of the matter rather than its imagined one.

The author, then, is not interested in how one should live, but in how one does live, in how the great men of

the past conducted their affairs, because, as he says in Chapter VI:

> . . . a prudent man should always take the path trodden by great men and imitate those who have been most outstanding; so that, if his own ingenuity does not come up to theirs, at least it will have the smell of it . . .

Machiavelli has no systematic theory of political morality, nor is he in search of one; in fact, he removes considerations of morality from the sphere of politics. The reader will notice how careful he is to stand at some distance from his characters and report on their actions, never moralizing on the "great men" he investigates.

Machiavelli wrote *The Prince* hastily in 1513 (perhaps between July and September), after he began working on the *Discourses on the First Ten Books of Titus Livy.* That the same man wrote two so dissimilar books has always disturbed some critics: the author of the *Discourses* emerges as an advocate of the republic while the author of *The Prince* advocates the principality. But the two works do not contradict each other if we see them as representing two different purposes: the one a treatise, the other a handbook.

How could the ideal republic hinted at in the *Discourses* possibly be realized in a politically chaotic and corrupt Italy? The sad condition of Italy in 1513 may have led Machiavelli to put aside theories and ideals and face the truth, the *"verità effettuale della cosa."* Strong leadership and organization, a redeemer to bring order to chaos, were necessary now if his ideal republic of the *Discourses* some day were to be realized. And so *The Prince*—a crying-out for action, for freedom from foreign domination, for reform and unification—was Machiavelli's answer to Italy's present needs. Because Machiavelli was seeking employment from the Medici when he wrote *The Prince,* dedi-

cating it to Lorenzo, does not mean that he wrote the book for self-aggrandizement. Only the opening dedication and some parts of the final chapter are meant to flatter the Medici; the intervening twenty-five chapters are devoid of any desire for selfish gain.

Not only the *Discourses* but Machiavelli's whole way of life make it clear that he considered a republic the best form of government, and the goal of human society the "common good." But the "effectual truth of the matter," things as they are, led him to advocate, through *The Prince*, the only kind of rule that he judged could serve his confused country during those desperate times.

Appearing frequently in all of Machiavelli's writings is that key word "*virtù*," which has posed problems for translator and critic alike. Scholars have tried their hand at defining "*virtù*" in a sentence or two, but no definition has caught its elusive significance. Most commentators are satisfied to call it "the human will in action"; Burkhardt's definition is more ambitious and elegant: "A union of force and ability, something that can be summed up in force alone, if, by force, one means human, not mechanical, force: will, and therefore force of ability."

There is no organized doctrine of "*virtù*" in the works of Machiavelli; the word must be examined and understood in its own special context, in the sentence or paragraph in which it occurs, and then, perhaps, it will reveal its particular meaning. I have found it necessary to use twelve different English words to translate "*virtù*," although many translators have been satisfied to render it as "virtue" in every instance. Only rarely does "virtue" capture the meaning Machiavelli intended. It may be helpful to list each instance in which the word appears, the number of times it is used in each chapter, and how I have chosen to translate it.

Chapter I

1. *et acquistonsi, o con le arme d' altri o con le proprie, o per fortuna o per virtù* / and they are acquired either with the arms of others or with one's own, either through fortune or through ingenuity

Chapter III

1. *di godere el benefizio del tempo, ma sì bene quello della virtù e prudenzia loro* / but rather they enjoyed the benefits of their ingenuity and prudence

Chapter IV

1. *Il che non è nato dalla molta o poca virtù del vincitore* / This does not come about from greater or lesser ingenuity on the part of the victor

Chapter VI

1. *né alla virtù di quelli che tu imiti aggiugnere* / nor arrive at the ingenuity of those they imitate
2. *acciò che, se la sua virtù non vi arriva, almeno ne renda qualche odore* / so that, if his own ingenuity does not come up to theirs, at least it will have the smell of it
3. *conoscendo fino a quanto va la virtù del loro arco* / aware of the capacity of their bow
4. *secondo che più o meno è virtuoso colui che gli acquista* / according to the greater or lesser ingenuity of the one who acquires them
5. *presuppone o virtù o fortuna* / presupposes either ingenuity or fortune
6. *che per propria virtù e non per fortuna* / by means of their own ingenuity and not by fortune
7. *e sanza quella occasione la virtù dello animo loro si sarebbe spenta* / and without that occasion their very ingenuity would have been extinguished
8. *e sanza quella virtù la occasione sarebbe venuto invano* / and without that ingenuity the occasion would have presented itself in vain
9. *Non posseva Teseo dimostrare la sua virtù* / Theseus could not have displayed his ingenuity

10. *e la eccellente virtù loro fece quella occasione essere co-nosciuta* / and their outstanding ingenuity made that occasion known to them
11. *e conviene che con la virtù li superino* / and they must overcome them by means of their ingenuity
12. *e fu di tanta virtù* / and he possessed so much ingenuity

Chapter VII
1. *se non è uomo di grande ingegno e virtù* / unless they are men of great talent and ingenuity
2. *sono di tanta virtù* / are of such ingenuity
3. *circa el diventare principe per virtù o per fortuna* / concerning becoming a prince by ingenuity or by fortune
4. *Francesco, per li debiti mezzi e con una grande sua virtù* / Francesco, with the proper means and great ingenuity
5. *facessi tutte quelle cose che per uno prudente e virtuoso uomo si dovea fare* / he did everything that a prudent and competent man should do
6. *potrebbe con una gran virtù farli poi* / could with great ingenuity do so later
7. *ma dalla potenzia e virtù sua* / but rather on his own power and ingenuity
8. *et era nel duca tanta ferocia e tanta virtù* / and there was in the duke such ferocity and such ingenuity

Chapter VIII
1. *o alla fortuna o alla virtù attribuire* / attributed altogether to fortune or ingenuity
2. *accompagnò le sua scelleratezze con tanta virtù d' animo e di corpo* / he coupled his iniquities with such ingenuity of mind and body
3. *Non si può ancora chiamare virtù* / Yet it cannot be called ingenuity
4. *Perché, se si considerassi la virtù di Agatocle* / For, if one were to consider the ingenuity of Agathocles
5. *Non si può adunque attribuire alla fortuna o alla virtù* / One cannot, therefore, attribute to fortune or ingenuity
6. *il quale aveva avuto maestro delle virtù e scelleratezze sua* / who had been his teacher in strategy and crime

Chapter IX

1. *nè a pervenirvi è necessario o tutta virtù o tutta fortuna* / the attainment of which depends neither entirely on ingenuity nor on fortune

Chapter XI

1. *o per virtù o per fortuna* / either through ingenuity or fortune
2. *con la bontà e infinite sue virtù* / through his bounty and infinite virtues

Chapter XII

1. *operorono virtuosissimamente* / they fought courageously
2. *lasciorono questa virtù* / they abandoned this strategy
3. *Et il fine della loro virtù* / And the effect of their ingenuity

Chapter XIII

1. *nelle ausiliarie la virtù* / with auxiliaries their courage
2. *con la sua fortuna e virtù* / by means of his good fortune and his ingenuity
3. *e tutta quella virtù* / and all that power
4. *non avendo virtù che nella avversità con fede lo diffenda* / not having the power and the loyalty to defend it in bad times

Chapter XIV

1. *Et è di tanta virtù* / And it is of such efficacy

Chapter XV

1. *si troverrà qualche cosa che parrà virtù* / he will discover that something that appears to be a virtue

Chapter XVI

1. *non potendo usare questa virtù del liberale* / unable to employ this virtue of generosity

Chapter XVII

1. *insieme con infinite sua virtù* / together with his many qualities

2. *le altre sua virtù non li bastavano* / his other qualities would not have been enough
3. *E che sia vero che l' altre sua virtù* / And that it is true that his other qualities

Chapter XIX
1. *e mostro grande virtù d' animo* / and displayed great strength of character
2. *accompagnato da molte virtù che lo facevano venerando* / endowed with many qualities that made him respected
3. *in Severo fu tanta virtù* / Severus possessed such ingenuity
4. *quelle sua virtù* / those qualities of his
5. *per non avere avuto tanta virtù* / since they did not possess enough ingenuity

Chapter XXI
1. *Debbe ancora uno principe mostrarsi amatore delle virtù* / A prince should show that he is an admirer of talent

Chapter XXIV
1. *che dependano da te proprio e dalla virtù tua* / that depend on yourself and on your own ingenuity

Chapter XXV
1. *dove non è ordinata virtù a resisterle* / where there is no prepared resources to resist her
2. *s'ella fussi reparata da conveniente virtù* / if she had been protected with suitable resources

Chapter XXVI
1. *e se ci era materia che dessi occasione a uno prudente e virtuoso* / and if there is the material that might afford one who is wise and ingenious the occasion
2. *la virtù di Moisè* / the capability of Moses
3. *volendo conoscere la virtù d'uno spirito italiano* / in order to recognize the capability of an Italian spirit
4. *con la sua fortuna e virtù* / with its fortune and ingenuity
5. *la virtù militare sia spenta* / her military strength is extinguished

6. *Qui è virtù grande nelle membra* / At present there is great strength in her members
7. *e per virtù e per fortuna* / by ingenuity and fortune
8. *per potere con la virtù italica* / so that with Italian strength
9. *Virtù contro a furore* / Ingenuity against rage

"Virtù" occurs fifty-nine times in *The Prince*; it appears three times as an adjective (*"virtuoso"*) and once as an adverb (*"virtuosissimamente"*). On seventeen occasions it is coupled with *"fortuna"* (which appears fifty-one times in the book), and in every such coupling it can be translated in its broader meaning of "ingenuity." The word "ingenuity" seemed the most appropriate choice because by definition it combines aptness and skill with inventive power and cleverness in originating and contriving, and I cannot help feeling that Machiavelli's Prince is, above all, a creative artist giving form to his material: creating a work of art, which is the principality, and like that of most artists, seldom perfect. I feel that "virtue" for *"virtù"* can be used only three times in *The Prince*: in Chapter XI, where it occurs in the plural, and in Chapters XV and XVI, where the word occurs only once in each chapter.

One thing seems certain: Machiavelli's *"virtù"* has nothing in common with the medieval passive concept of *"virtù"* involving contemplation and prayer; indeed, it is the reverse: a concept of action involving both mind and body. And when it is not specifically *capacity, strategy, virtue, courage, power, efficacy, qualities, strength, talent, resources,* or *capability,* then it is *ingenuity,* a general term broad enough by its own definition to suggest some of the eleven more specific meanings of *"virtù."*

My translation, unlike many recent ones, was not intended to make Machiavelli sound like a twentieth-century journalist. I have not broken his long and often involved sentences into a number of shorter ones, for

Machiavelli develops and extends an idea in the course of a sentence, juxtaposing not only important words but also phrases and entire clauses, sometimes for dramatic effect and sometimes for didactic reasons. His longer sentences can be confusing: his enthusiasm will overwhelm both his logic and grammar, and a translation should be faithful to the changes in tone and intensity. *The Prince* is by no means Machiavelli's most polished work, but, then, he did not mean it to be:

I have neither adorned nor filled this book with polished sentences, with rich and magnificent words, or with any other kind of rhetorical or superfluous ornamentation, the likes of which many writers are accustomed to using in describing and embellishing their material; for it was my desire that nothing distinguish my book or make it pleasing other than the unusualness of its material and the importance of its contents exclusively. . . .

Note on the Text

Although manuscript copies of *The Prince* were circulated shortly after the work was completed toward the end of 1513, it was not published until after Machiavelli's death. The first edition appeared in Rome in 1532; it was edited by Antonio Blado, who got permission from Pope Clement VII to publish all of Machiavelli's works. *The Prince*, with several of the author's other compositions, was also published in Florence by Bernardo di Giunta in the same year and again in 1540. Between 1537 and 1554 at least six editions were printed in Venice. The first edition of the collected works of Machiavelli appeared in 1550, and the first Latin translation, by which the work became known in other countries, was done in 1560, after which it was quickly translated into French, English, German, and Swedish.

The Italian text used in this edition is the one prepared by Mario Casella and published in Rome (1930) by Libreria d'Italia.

A note of thanks to my friend Professor Gerald Strauss of the History Department of Indiana University for reading my translation and making suggestions, to the students in my seminar on *Machiavelli and the Renaissance*, who read parts of the translation and often made valuable suggestions, and to Miss Catherine Blanchard for her assistance in the preparation of the final manuscript and for reminding me that the English language can do just so much. Special thanks to my editor, Joan Levinson, for all her kindness and *per le altre sua virtù*.

Selected Bibliography

EDITIONS

Il Principe. Ed. by L. Arthur Burd. Oxford: Clarendon Press, 1891.

Il Principe. Ed. by Giuseppe Lisio. Florence: Sansoni, 1900.

Il Principe. Ed. by Luigi Firpo, with introduction and notes by Federico Chabod. Torino: Einaudi, 1962.

Il Principe. Ed. by Mario Casella. Rome: Libreria d'Italia, 1930.

Opere. Ed. by Antonio Panella. 2 vols. Milan: Rizzoli, 1938.

Opere. Ed. by Mario Bonfantini. Milan: Ricciardi, 1954.

STUDIES

Baron, Hans. "*The Prince* and the Puzzle of the Date of the *Discorsi*," in *Bibliothèque d'Humanisme et Renaissance.* Vol. LXXVI, 1961. 217-253.

Butterfield, Herbert. *The Statecraft of Machiavelli.* London, 1940.

Chabod, Federico. *Machiavelli and the Renaissance,* tr. by David Moore, Cambridge, Mass.: Harvard University Press, 1960.

Chabod, Federico. *Scritti su Machiavelli.* Torino: Einaudi, 1964.

Hale, J. R. *Machiavelli and Renaissance Italy.* New York: Macmillan, 1960.

Macaulay, Thomas B. "Machiavelli." *The Proper Study*. New York: St Martin's Press, 1962.

Maritain, Jacques. "The End of Machiavellianism." *The Review of Politics*. Vol. IV, January, 1942.

Mattingly, Garret. "Machiavelli's *Prince*: Political Science or Political Satire?" *The American Scholar*. Vol. XXVII, 1958.

Olschki, Leonardo. *Machiavelli, the Scientist*. Berkeley: University of California Press, 1945.

Prezzolini, Giuseppe. *Machiavelli Anticristo*. Rome: Gherardo Casini, 1954.

Ridolfi, Roberto. *The Life of Niccolò Machiavelli*, tr. by Cecil Grayson. Chicago: University of Chicago Press, 1963.

Roeder, Ralph. *The Man of the Renaissance*. New York: Meridian Books, 1960.

Russo, Luigi. *Machiavelli*. Bari: Laterza, 1957.

Sasso, Gennaro. *Niccolò Machiavelli, Storia del Suo Pensiero Politico*. Naples: Istituto Italiano Per Gli Studi Storici, 1958.

Strauss, Leo. *Thoughts on Machiavelli*. Glencoe: Free Press, 1958.

Indice

Contents

Nicolaus Maclavellus ad Magnificum

Sogliono, el più delle volte, coloro che desiderano acquistare grazia appresso uno Principe, farseli incontro con
quelle cose che infra le loro abbino più care, o delle quali
vegghino lui più delettarsi; donde si vede molte volte
essere loro presentati cavalli, arme, drappi d' oro, pietre
preziose e simili ornamenti degni della grandezza di quelli.
Desiderando io, adunque, offerirmi alla Vostra Magnificenzia con qualche testimone della servitù mia verso di
quella, non ho trovato, intra la mia suppellettile, cosa
quale io abbi più cara o tanto esistimi quanto la cognizione delle azioni delli uomini grandi, imparata da me
con una lunga esperienza delle cose moderne e una continua lezione delle antique; le quali avendo io con gran
diligenzia lungamente escogitate ed esaminate, e ora in
uno piccolo volume ridotte, mando alla Magnificenzia
Vostra.

E benchè io guidichi questa opera indegna della pre-
senzia di quella, tamen confido assai che per sua umanità
li debba essere accetta, considerato come da me non li
possa essere fatto maggiore dono che darle facultà a
potere in brevissimo tempo intendere tutto quello che
io, in tanti anni e con tanti mia disagi e periculi, ho
conosciuto e inteso. La quale opera io non ho ornata nè
ripiena di clausule ample o di parole ampullose e magni-
fiche, o di qualunque altro lenocinio o ornamento estrin-
seco, con li quali molti sogliono le loro cose descrivere e
ornare: perchè io ho voluto, o che veruna cosa la onori, o
che solamente la varietà della materia e la gravità del
subietto la facci grata. Nè voglio sia reputata presunzione
se uno uomo di basso ed infimo stato ardisce discorrere e

Niccolò Machiavelli to the Magnificent

LORENZO DE' MEDICI[1]

It is customary, in most cases, for those who desire to win the favor of a Prince to present themselves to him with those things they cherish most or which they know please him most; hence, we often see Princes[2] presented with horses, arms, gold vestments, precious stones and similar adornments worthy of their greatness. Desiring, then, to offer myself to Your Magnificence with some proof of my devotion to you, I have not found among my possessions anything that I cherish more or value so much as my knowledge of the accomplishments of great men, which I learned through long experience in contemporary affairs and continuous study of antiquity; having very diligently and for a long time thought about and analyzed these accomplishments, and now having condensed them into a little book, I am sending them to Your Magnificence.

And although I regard this work unworthy of your consideration, I am nevertheless quite confident that your kindness will convince you to accept it, for I could not make you a greater gift than to give you the means to be able in very short time to understand all that which I, over many years[3] and with many difficulties and dangers, came to know and understand. I have neither adorned nor filled this book with polished sentences, with rich and magnificent words, or with any other kind of rhetorical or superfluous ornamentation, the likes of which many writers are accustomed to using in describing and embellishing their material; for it was my desire that nothing distinguish my book or make it pleasing other than the unusualness of its material and the importance of its con-

1

regolare e' governi de' principi; perchè, così come coloro
che disegnano e paesi si pongono bassi nel piano a considerare la natura de' monti e de' luoghi alti e, per considerare quella de' bassi, si pongono alti sopra e monti;
similmente, a conoscere bene la natura de' populi, bisogna essere principe, e a conoscere bene quella de' principi, bisogna essere populare.

Pigli, adunque, Vostra Magnificenzia questo piccolo
dono con quello animo che io lo mando; el quale se da
quella fia diligentemente considerato e letto, vi conoscerà
drento uno estremo mio desiderio, che Lei pervenga a
quella grandezza che la fortuna e le altre sue qualità li
promettano. E se Vostra Magnificenzia dallo apice della
sua altezza qualche volta volgerà gli occhi in questi luoghi
bassi, conoscerà quanto io indegnamente sopporti una
grande e continua malignità di fortuna.

tents exclusively. I hope it will not be thought presump-
tuous if a man of low and inferior station dare to debate
and regulate the government of princes; for, just as those
persons who sketch landscapes place themselves in a low
position on the plain in order to study the nature of the
mountains and highlands, and in order to study the low-
lands place themselves high on top of the mountains, in
like fashion, in order to know well the nature of the peo-
ple one must be a prince, and to know well the nature of
princes one must be a common citizen.

Accept then, Your Magnificence, this little gift in the
spirit that I send it; and if you deign to consider and read
it with care, you will discover in it my utmost desire that
you may reach that greatness which fortune and your own
capacities predict for you. And if Your Magnificence from
the summit of his high position will at some time move
his eyes toward these lowlands, he will know to what
extent I unjustly endure the great and continuous malefi-
cence of fortune.

NOTES

1. Lorenzo de' Medici (1492–1519), not to be confused with Lorenzo the Magnificent, succeeded Giuliano as ruler of Florence in 1513. *The Prince* had first been dedicated to Giuliano de' Medici, who ruled Florence from 1512–1513 and died in 1516. Machiavelli changed the dedication before 1517.

2. The plural "loro" would seem to arise from "uno Principe" in line 2: a casual switch from the singular to the plural (not easily rendered in English) is often found in Machiavelli's longer and involved sentences. Machiavelli is more concerned with what he says than how he says it.

3. Machiavelli was about forty-three when he wrote *The Prince.*

De Principatibus

I Quot Sint Genera Principatuum et Quibus Modis Acquirantur

Tutti gli stati, tutti e dominii che hanno avuto e hanno imperio sopra li uomini, sono stati e sono o republiche o principati. E principati sono: o ereditarii, de' quali el sangue del loro signore ne sia suto lungo tempo principe, o sono nuovi. E nuovi, o e' sono nuovi tutti, come fu Milano a Francesco Sforza, o e' sono come membri aggiunti allo stato ereditario del principe che li acquista, come è el regno di Napoli al re di Spagna. Sono questi dominii così acquistati, o consueti a vivere sotto uno principe, o usi ad essere liberi; e acquistonsi o con le armi d'altri o con le proprie, o per fortuna o per virtù.

On Principalities

I How Many Types of Principalities There Are and the Way They Are Acquired

All the states, all the dominions that have had and still have power over men, were and still are either republics or principalities. Principalities are either hereditary, in which case the family of the prince has been ruling for generations, or they are new. And the new ones are either completely new, as was Milan for Francesco Sforza,[1] or they are like members joined to the hereditary state of the prince who acquires them, as is the kingdom of Naples for the King of Spain.[2] Dominions acquired in this manner are either accustomed to living under a prince or used to being free; and they are acquired either with the arms of others or with one's own, either through fortune or through ingenuity.

NOTES

1. Francesco Sforza (1401–1466), the son of Muzio Attendolo, married the daughter (Maria Bianca) of Filippo Maria Visconti, Duke of Milan; at the latter's death Milan became a republic with Sforza at the head of the army, who, instead of defending Milan from the Venetians, secretly allied himself with them; then turning against the Ambrosian Republic, he took possession of Milan and declared himself her ruler in 1450.

2. Ferdinand the Catholic, King of Spain, had agreed upon the sharing of the reign of Naples with Louis XII in the Treaty of Granada (November 11, 1500); but Ferdinand broke the pact and stripped his ally of his share by reuniting Naples and Sicily to Spain with the title of Vicereame in 1504.

II De Principatibus Hereditariis

Io lascerò indrieto el ragionare delle republiche, perchè altra volta ne ragionai a lungo. Volteròmmi solo al principato, e andrò tessendo li orditi soprascritti, e disputerò come questi principati si possino governare e mantenere.

Dico, adunque, che nelli stati ereditarii e assuefatti al sangue del loro principe sono assai minori difficultà a mantenerli che ne' nuovi; perchè basta solo non preterire l' ordine de' sua antenati e, di poi, temporeggiare con gli accidenti; in modo che, se tale principe è di ordinaria industria, sempre si manterrà nel suo stato, se non è una estraordinaria ed eccessiva forza che ne lo privi; e, privato che ne fia, quantunque di sinistro abbi lo occupatore, lo riacquista.

Noi abbiamo in Italia, in exemplis, el duca di Ferrara; il quale non ha retto alli assalti de' Viniziani nello '84, nè a quelli di papa Iulio nel '10, per altre cagioni che per essere antiquato in quello dominio. Perchè el principe naturale ha minori cagioni e minore necessità di offendere; donde conviene che sia più amato; e se estraordinarii vizii non lo fanno odiare, è ragionevole che naturalmente sia benevoluto da' sua. E nella antiquità e continuazione del dominio sono spente le memorie e le cagioni delle innovazioni; perchè sempre una mutazione lascia l' addentellato per la edificazione dell' altra.

NOTES

1. A reference to the first book of the *Discourses*, which was written before *The Prince*.

2. Machiavelli alludes to the two dukes of Ferrara: Ercole d'Este (1471–1505), defeated by the Venetians, and his successor, Alfonso d'Este, who was allied with Louis XII in the war of the Lega Santa (1510–1512) and, as a result, was banished

II On Hereditary Principalities

I shall put aside any discussion of republics, since I discussed them at length once before.[1] I shall treat only the principality, developing as I go the outline mentioned above; and I shall argue how these principalities may be governed and maintained.

Let me say, then, that in hereditary states accustomed to the rule of their prince's family there are far fewer difficulties in maintaining them than in the new ones; for it would suffice simply not to transgress the ancestral practices, and then to adjust one's self according to unforeseen events; in this way, if such a prince is of average ability, he will always rule in his state, unless some unusual and inordinate force deprive him of it; and although he may be deprived of it, with the slightest mishap to the occupier, he will reclaim it.

We have in Italy, as an example, the Duke of Ferrara,[2] who held up against the assaults of the Venetians in 1484 and of Pope Julius in 1510 for no other reason than his ancestral reign in that dominion. Since a prince by birth has fewer reasons and less need to offend his subjects, it follows that he should be more loved, and if he has no extraordinary vices to make him hateful, it is understandable why he is naturally well liked by them. And in the antiquity and duration of his reign memories and the reasons for innovations are extinguished, because one change always leaves a denticulation[3] for the construction of another.

from the state for a time by Pope Julius II, who was against the King of France.

3. The word *addentellato* is a technical architectural term referring to a toothed wall left on a building so that another building may be built on to it. In light of the word *edificazione* ("construction") which follows, *addentellato* proves to be an effective word choice here.

7

Ma nel principato nuovo consistono le difficultà. E prima, se non è tutto nuovo, ma come membro (che si può chiamare tutto insieme quasi misto) le variazioni sua nascono in prima da una naturale difficultà, quale è in tutti e principati nuovi: le quali sono che li uomini mutono volentieri signore credendo megliorare; e questa credenza gli fa pigliare l'arme contro a quello; di che e' s'ingannono, perchè veggono poi per esperienzia avere peggiorato. Il che depende da una altra necessità naturale e ordinaria, quale fa che sempre bisogni offendere quelli di chi si diventa nuovo principe e con gente d'arme e con infinite altre iniurie che si tira drieto el nuovo acquisto; in modo che tu hai inimici tutti quelli che hai offesi in occupare quello principato, e non ti puoi mantenere amici quelli che vi ti hanno messo, per non li potere satisfare in quel modo che si erano presupposto, e per non potere tu usare contro a di loro medicine forti, sendo loro obligato; perchè sempre, ancora che uno sia fortissimo in su li eserciti, ha bisogno del favore de' provinciali a intrare in una provincia. Per queste cagioni Luigi xii re di Francia occupò subito Milano, e subito lo perdè; e bastò a torgnene, la prima volta, le forze proprie di Lodovico; perchè quelli populi che gli avevano aperte le porte, trovandosi ingannati della opinione loro e di quello futuro bene che si avevano presupposto, non potevono sopportare e fastidii del nuovo principe.

È ben vero che, acquistandosi poi la seconda volta e paesi rebellati, si perdono con più difficultà; perchè il signore, presa occasione dalla rebellione, è meno respettivo ad assicurarsi con punire e' delinquenti, chiarire e suspetti, provvedersi nelle parte più debole. In modo che, se a fare perdere Milano a Francia bastò, la prima volta, uno duca Lodovico che romoreggiassi in su e confini, a farlo di poi

III On Mixed Principalities

But it is with the new principality that difficulties arise.[1] First, if it is not altogether new but rather an addition (so that the two together may be called mixed), its problems originate mainly from one inherent difficulty that exists in all new principalities: men willingly change masters, believing to better themselves; and this belief makes them take up arms against their master, but in this they deceive themselves, because eventually with experience they see that things have gotten worse. Problems stem from another natural and common necessity, which is that a prince will always offend his new subjects both with his soldiers and with the many other abuses that accompany his new conquest; as a result you have made enemies of all those you offended while occupying that principality, and you are not able to keep those friends that helped to put you in power, since you are incapable of satisfying them in the way they had expected, nor can you use drastic measures[2] against them, for you are obligated to them; because, though one may have the strongest of armies, one always needs the backing of the inhabitants to take over a province. For these reasons Louis XII, King of France,[3] quickly occupied Milan and quickly lost it; and the first time Ludovico's[4] troops alone were enough to take it from him, because those people who had opened the gates to him, finding themselves deceived in their beliefs and in that future good they had anticipated, could not put up with the affronts of the new prince.

It is certainly true that once those lands that have rebelled are conquered a second time, they are lost with more difficulty; for the master, taking advantage of the rebellion, is less hesitant in insuring his position by punishing offenders, exposing suspects, and strengthening himself in weak spots. So that, if in order for France to lose Milan the first time, only the person of a Duke Ludovico

perdere, la seconda, gli bisognò avere contro el mondo tutto, e che li eserciti suoi fussino spenti o fugati di Italia; il che nacque dalle cagioni sopradette. Nondimanco, e la prima e la seconda volta, li fu tolto.

Le cagioni universali della prima si sono discorse; resta ora a dire quelle della seconda, e vedere che remedii lui ci aveva, e quali ci può avere uno che fussi ne' termini sua, per potersi meglio mantenere nello acquisto che non fece Francia. Dico, pertanto, che questi stati, quali acquistandosi si aggiungono a uno stato antiquo di quello che acquista, o e' sono della medesima provincia e della medesima lingua, o non sono. Quando e' sieno, è facilità grande a tenerli, massime quando non sieno usi a vivere liberi; e a possederli securamente basta avere spenta la linea del principe che li dominava, perchè nelle altre cose, mantenendosi loro le condizioni vecchie e non vi essendo disformità di costumi, gli uomini si vivono quietamente; come si è visto che ha fatto la Borgogna, la Brettagna, la Guascogna e la Normandia, che tanto tempo sono state con Francia; e benchè vi sia qualche disformità di lingua, nondimeno e' costumi sono simili, e possonsi fra loro facilmente comportare. E chi le acquista, volendole tenere, debbe avere dua respetti: l'uno, che il sangue del loro principe antiquo si spenga; l'altro, di non alterare nè loro legge nè loro dazii; talmente che in brevissimo tempo diventa, con loro principato antiquo, tutto uno corpo.

Ma quando si acquista stati in una provincia disforme di lingua, di costumi e di ordini, qui sono le difficultà, e

threatening the borders was enough, in order to cause her to lose it a second time, the whole world[5] had to oppose her and wipe out her armies or drive them out of Italy; and this came about for the reasons mentioned above. In spite of this, both the first and second time it was taken away from her.

The general reasons for the first loss have been discussed; there remains to mention those for the second, and to see what solutions there were for the King of France, and those available to one who might be in the same situation, so that he might be able to keep a better hold over his conquest than did France. I say, then, that those dominions that once conquered are annexed to the long-established state of the conqueror are either of the same province and language or they are not. When they are, it is very easy to hold on to them, especially so when they are not accustomed to freedom; and to possess them securely one need only to have extinguished the family line of the former prince in power, because as far as other things are concerned, so long as their old way of life is preserved and there is no difference in customs, men will live peacefully: as we have seen in the case of Burgundy, Brittany, Gascony and Normandy,[6] which have been joined to France for so long a time; and although there is a certain dissimilarity in the language, nonetheless the customs are the same, and they have been able to get along together easily. And whoever takes possession of such lands and desires to hold on to them should keep two things in mind: the first, that the family line of the old prince must be extinguished; the other, that neither the laws nor the taxes be changed; as a result in a very short time they will become, together with the old principality, as one body.

But when dominions are acquired in a province that differs in language, customs and laws, it is here that diffi-

qui bisogna avere gran fortuna e grande industria a tenerli. E uno de' maggiori remedii e più vivi sarebbe che la persona di chi acquista vi andassi ad abitare. Questo farebbe più secura e più durabile quella possessione: come ha fatto el Turco, di Grecia: il quale, con tutti gli altri ordini osservati da lui per tenere quello stato, se non vi fussi ito ad abitare, non era possibile che lo tenessi. Perchè, standovi, si veggono nascere e disordini, e presto vi puoi rimediare; non vi stando, s'intendono quando e' sono grandi e che non vi è più remedio. Non è, oltre di questo, la provincia spogliata da' tua officiali; satisfannosi e' sudditi del ricorso propinquo al principe; donde hanno più cagione di amarlo volendo essere buoni e, volendo essere altrimenti, di temerlo. Chi delli esterni volessi assaltare quello stato, vi ha più respetto; tanto che, abitandovi, lo può con grandissima difficultà perdere.

L'altro migliore remedio è mandare colonie in uno o in dua luoghi, che sieno quasi compedes di quello stato; perchè è necessario o fare questo o tenervi assai gente d'arme e fanti. Nelle colonie non si spende molto; e sanza sua spesa, o poca, ve le manda e tiene; e solamente offende coloro a chi e' toglie e campi e le case per darle a' nuovi abitatori, che sono una minima parte di quello stato; e quelli che gli offende, rimanendo dispersi e poveri, non gli possono mai nuocere, e tutti li altri rimangono da uno canto inoffesi (e per questo doverrebbono quietarsi), dall'altro paurosi di non errare, per timore che non intervenissi a loro come a quelli che sono stati spogliati. Concludo che queste colonie non costano, sono più fedeli, offendono meno; e gli offesi non possono nuocere, sendo

culties arise; and in this case one needs a great deal of good fortune and much zeal to hold on to them. And one of the best and most effective solutions would be for the person who has taken possession to go there to live. This move would make that possession more secure and more permanent: just as the Turk did with Greece;[7] for in spite of all the other precautions he took to hold on to that dominion, if he had not gone there to live, it would have been impossible for him to hold it. Because, living right there, one sees trouble from its start and can take care of it immediately; not living there, one hears about it when it has greatly increased and there is no longer any remedy. Besides this, the province would not be plundered by one's officials; the subjects would be satisfied in having direct recourse to the prince; this way, desiring to be good citizens, they have more reason to love him, and, desiring to be otherwise, more reason to fear him. Whatever outside force might want to invade that dominion would be more hesitant in undertaking it; so that the prince, living right there, can only with the greatest difficulty lose it.

The other and even better solution is to send colonies into one or two places that will serve as connecting links to your state; for it is imperative that either the prince do this or maintain a large cavalry and infantry. Colonies do not cost much, and at little or no cost on the part of the prince, he can send and maintain them; and he only hurts those whose fields and houses are taken and given to the new inhabitants, who are a very small part of that state; and those that he hurts, scattered and poor as they are, can never be a threat to him, and all the others remain on the one hand unharmed (and therefore they should be quiet), and on the other fearful of making a mistake, lest what happened to those who had been dispossessed might happen to them. I conclude that these colonies are

poveri e dispersi, come è detto. Per il che si ha a notare che li uomini si debbano o vezzeggiare o spegnere; perchè si vendicano delle leggieri offese, delle gravi non possono; sì che l'offesa che si fa all'uomo debba essere in modo che la non tema la vendetta. Ma tenendovi, in cambio di colonie, gente d'arme, si spende più assai, avendo a consumare nella guardia tutte le intrate di quello stato; in modo che lo acquisto li torna perdita; e offende molto più, perchè nuoce a tutto quello stato, tramutando con gli alloggiamenti il suo esercito; del quale disagio ognuno ne sente, e ciascuno gli diventa inimico; e sono inimici che li possono nuocere, rimanendo, battuti, in casa loro. Da ogni parte, dunque, questa guardia è inutile, come quella delle colonie è utile.

Debbe ancora chi è in una provincia disforme come è detto, farsi capo e defensore de' vicini minori potenti, ed ingegnarsi di indebolire e potenti di quella, e guardarsi che, per accidente alcuno, non vi entri uno forestiere potente quanto lui. E sempre interverrà che vi sarà messo da coloro che saranno in quella mal contenti o per troppa ambizione o per paura: come si vidde già che li Etoli missono e Romani in Grecia; e in ogni altra provincia che gli entrorono, vi furono messi da' provinciali. E l'ordine delle cose è che, subito che uno forestiere potente entra in una provincia, tutti quelli che sono in essa meno potenti gli aderiscano, mossi da una invidia hanno contro a chi è suto potente sopra di loro; tanto che, respetto a questi minori potenti, lui non ha a durare fatica alcuna a guadagnarli, perchè subito tutti insieme voluntieri fanno uno globo col suo stato che lui vi ha acquistato. Ha solamente a pensare che non piglino troppe forze e troppa

not expensive, they are more faithful, and they give less trouble; and those who are hurt can pose no threat, since they are poor and scattered, as I have said. About this it should be noted that men must be either pampered or done away with, because they will revenge themselves for a slight hurt, but for serious ones they cannot; so that any hurt done to a man should be the kind that leaves no fear of revenge. But by maintaining, instead of colonies, an army of men, one spends much more, for all the revenues of that state will be used up in guarding it, so that the gain turns into a loss; and far greater injury is done, because the whole state is hurt by the prince's army changing quarters from one place to another; everyone feels this inconvenience, and everyone becomes an enemy; and they are enemies that can do harm, for they remain, though conquered, in their own home. In every respect, therefore, this kind of defense is as useless as the other kind, the founding of colonies, is useful.

Furthermore, whoever is in a province that differs from his own in the ways just mentioned should make himself the head and protector of his less powerful neighbors and do all possible to weaken those who are strong, and he should be on his guard that, for whatever reason, no foreigner as powerful as himself enter there. And it will always happen that the foreigner will be brought in by those who are dissatisfied because of either excessive ambition or fear: as was seen once when the Aetolians brought the Romans into Greece;[8] and every other province the Romans entered, they were brought in by the inhabitants. What happens is that as soon as a powerful foreigner enters a province, all those who are less powerful cling to him, impelled by their envy of the one who has ruled over them; so that, in regard to these weaker powers, he has no difficulty whatever in winning them over, for all of them will immediately and gladly blend into the state

autorità; e facilmente può, con le forze sua e col favore
loro, sbassare quelli che sono potenti, per rimanere, in
tutto, arbitro di quella provincia. E chi non governerà
bene questa parte, perderà presto quello arà acquistato e,
mentre che lo terrà, vi arà, drento, infinite difficultà e
fastidii.

E Romani, nelle provincie che pigliorono, osservorono
bene queste parti; e mandorono le colonie, intrattenneno
e meno potenti sanza crescere loro potenzia, abbassorono
e potenti, e non vi lasciorono prendere reputazione
a' potenti forestieri. E voglio mi basti solo la provincia di
Grecia per esemplo: furno intrattenuti da loro gli Achei
e gli Etoli; fu abbassato el regno de' Macedoni; funne
cacciato Antioco; nè mai e meriti degli Achei o degli Etoli
feciono che permettessero loro accrescere alcuno stato;
nè le persuasioni di Filippo li indussono mai ad esserli
amici sanza sbassarlo; nè la potenza di Antioco possè fare
li consentissero che tenessi in quella provincia alcuno
stato. Perchè e Romani feciono in questi casi quello che
tutti e principi savii debbano fare: e quali, non solamente
hanno ad avere riguardo alli scandoli presenti, ma
a' futuri, e a quelli con ogni industria obviare; perchè, pre-
vedendosi discosto, facilmente vi si può rimediare, ma, as-
pettando che ti si appressino, la medicina non è a tempo,
perchè la malattia è divenuta incurabile. E interviene di
questa come dicono e fisici dello etico, che, nel principio
del suo male, è facile e curare e difficile a conoscere, ma,
nel progresso del tempo, non l'avendo in principio conosciuta nè medicata, diventa facile a conoscere e difficile a
curare. Così interviene nelle cose di stato; perchè, conoscendo discosto (il che non è dato se non a uno prudente)
e mali che nascono in quello, si guariscono presto; ma

he has taken over. He has only to beware that they do not get hold of too much power and authority; and he can very easily, with his strength and their backing, put down those who are powerful, remaining, in everything, arbiter of that province. And whoever does not follow carefully this practice will soon lose what he has acquired; and while he holds it he will find it full of infinite difficulties and troubles.

In the provinces they took over, the Romans carefully followed these practices; they sent in colonies, kept the less powerful in check without increasing their strength, put down the powerful, and did not allow powerful foreigners to gain prestige there. And I shall let the province of Greece serve as my only example: the Romans kept a friendly check on the Achaeans and the Aetolians; the kingdom of Macedonia was put down; Antiochus[9] was driven out; nor were they ever induced by the merits of the Achaeans or the Aetolians to allow them any gain of territory; nor did the coaxing of Philip ever convince them to make him a friend without first putting him down; nor could the power of Antiochus make them consent to his holding any authority at all in that province. For the Romans did in these cases what all wise princes should do: they not only have to watch out for troubles at hand, but also for those ahead, and endeavor diligently to avoid them; for once trouble is foreseen, it can be easily remedied; however, if you wait for it to become evident, the medicine will be too late, for the disease will have become incurable. And what doctors say about a disease will apply here: that at the beginning the disease is easy to cure but difficult to recognize; but, as time goes on, not having at the start been recognized or treated, it becomes easy to recognize and difficult to cure. The same thing happens in affairs of state; for recognizing from afar

quando, per non li avere conosciuti, si lasciano crescere in modo che ognuno li conosce, non vi è più remedio.

Però e Romani, vedendo discosto gli inconvenienti, vi rimediorno sempre; e non li lasciorno mai seguire per fuggire una guerra, perchè sapevano che la guerra non si leva, ma si differisce a vantaggio di altri; però vollono fare con Filippo e Antioco guerra in Grecia, per non la avere a fare con loro in Italia; e potevano per allora fuggire l' una e l' altra; il che non volsero. Nè piacque mai loro quello che tutto dì è in bocca de' savii de' nostri tempi, di godere el beneficio del tempo, ma sì bene quello della virtù e prudenzia loro; perchè il tempo si caccia innanzi ogni cosa, e può condurre seco bene come male e male come bene.

Ma torniamo a Francia, ed esaminiamo se delle cose dette ne ha fatto alcuna; e parlerò di Luigi, e non di Carlo, come di colui che, per avere tenuta più lunga possessione in Italia, si sono meglio visti e sua progressi; e vedrete come egli ha fatto el contrario di quelle cose che si debbono fare per tenere uno stato in una provincia disforme.

El re Luigi fu messo in Italia dalla ambizione de' Viniziani, che volsero guadagnarsi mezzo lo stato di Lombardia per quella venuta. Io non voglio biasimare questo partito preso dal re; perchè, volendo cominciare a mettere uno piè in Italia, e non avendo in questa provincia amici, anzi sendoli, per li portamenti del re Carlo, serrate tutte le porte, fu forzato prendere quelle amicizie che poteva; e sarebbeli riuscito el partito ben preso, quando nelli altri maneggi non avessi fatto errore alcuno. Acquistata, adun-

(which is the gift of only a prudent ruler) the disorders that are taking form within, one can soon heal them; but when, not having been recognized, they are left to grow so that everyone recognizes them, there is no longer a remedy.

For this reason the Romans, sensing trouble from afar, always found a remedy; and they never allowed it to develop in order to avoid going to war, because they knew that war cannot be avoided but only postponed to the advantage of others; therefore, they decided to go to war with Philip and Antiochus in Greece in order not to have to fight them in Italy; and they could have, for the time being, avoided both the one and the other, but they did not want to. Nor did they ever like what is constantly on the lips of our sages today, to enjoy the benefits of the present time, but rather they enjoyed the benefits of their ingenuity and prudence; for time brings out everything, and it can bring with it the good as well as the bad and the bad as well as the good.

But let us return to France and see if she did any of the things just mentioned; and I shall talk about Louis, not Charles,[10] and so about him whose development has been observed better because he held possession in Italy for a longer time:[11] and you will see that he did the opposite of those things that must be done in order to maintain one's rule in a foreign country.

King Louis was brought into Italy by the ambition of the Venetians, who by his coming wanted to win for themselves half of Lombardy.[12] I do not wish to condemn the enterprise undertaken by the king; for desiring to get a first foothold in Italy and having no friends in this country—furthermore, because of the actions of King Charles all the gates were closed to him—he was forced to make whatever friends he could; and this worthwhile enterprise would have been successful if he had not made any mis-

que, el re la Lombardia, si riguadagnò subito quella reputazione che gli aveva tolta Carlo: Genova cedè; e Fiorentini li diventorno amici; marchese di Mantova, duca di
Ferrara, Bentivogli, madonna di Furlì, signore di Faenza,
di Pesaro, di Rimino, di Camerino, di Piombino, Lucchesi,
Pisani, Sanesi, ognuno se li fece incontro per essere suo
amico. E allora posserno considerare e Viniziani la teme-
rità del partito preso da loro; e quali, per acquistare dua
terre in Lombardia, fecioro signore, el re, del terzo di
Italia.

Consideri ora uno con quanta poca difficultà posseva
il re tenere in Italia la sua reputazione, se egli avessi
osservate le regole soprascritte e tenuti securi e difesi tutti
quelli sua amici, e quali, per essere gran numero, e deboli,
e paurosi chi della Chiesa chi de' Viniziani, erano sempre
necessitati a stare seco; e per il mezzo loro posseva facilmente assicurarsi di chi ci restava grande. Ma lui non
prima fu in Milano, che fece il contrario, dando aiuto a
papa Alessandro perchè elli occupassi la Romagna. Nè
si accorse, con questa deliberazione, che faceva sè debole,
togliendosi gli amici e quelli che se li erano gittati in
grembo, e la Chiesa grande, aggiungendo allo spirituale,
che li dà tanto autorità, tanto temporale. E fatto uno
primo errore, fu costretto a seguitare; in tanto che, per
porre fine alla ambizione di Alessandro, e perchè non
divenissi signore di Toscana, fu costretto venire in Italia.
Non li bastò avere fatto grande la Chiesa e toltisi li amici,
che, per volere il regno di Napoli, lo divise con il re di
Spagna; e dove lui era, prima, arbitro d' Italia, e' vi misse
uno compagno, acciò che li ambiziosi di quella provincia
e mal contenti di lui avessino dove ricorrere; e dove posseva lasciare in quello regno uno re suo pensionario, e'
ne lo trasse, per mettervi uno che potessi cacciarne lui.

takes in his other manoeuvres. The King, then, having taken over Lombardy, immediately won back that prestige which Charles had taken from him: Genoa surrendered; the Florentines became his friends; the marquis of Mantua, the duke of Ferrara, the Bentivogli, the Countess of Forlì, lords of Faenza, of Pesaro, of Rimini, of Camerino, of Piombino, the people of Lucca, Pisa, and Siena, all came to him in friendship.[14] And then the Venetians were able to see the imprudence of the enterprise they had undertaken; in order to acquire a few cities in Lombardy, they made the King master of a third of Italy.

Now think with what little difficulty the King could have maintained his prestige in Italy if he had observed the rules mentioned above and kept safe and secure all those friends of his, who, there being a large number of them, both weak and fearful, some of the Church, others of the Venetians, were bound by necessity to stay by his side; and by means of them he could easily have protected himself from those who remained great powers. But no sooner was he in Milan than he did the opposite, helping Pope Alexander to occupy the Romagna.[15] Nor did he realize that with this move he weakened himself, stripping himself of his friends and of those who had thrown themselves into his lap, and made the Church stronger by adding so much temporal power to the spiritual power that gives it so much authority. And having made one mistake, he was forced to continue making others; so that in order to put an end to the ambition of Alexander, that he might not become master of Tuscany, he was forced to come to Italy. He was not satisfied to have made the Church powerful and to have stripped himself of his friends, for desiring the kingdom of Naples, he divided it with the King of Spain;[16] and, whereas at one time he was arbiter of Italy, he brought in a companion

È cosa veramente molto naturale e ordinaria desiderare
di acquistare; e sempre, quando li uomini lo fanno che
possono, saranno laudati o non biasimati; ma, quando e'
non possono e vogliono farlo in ogni modo, qui è lo
errore e il biasimo. Se Francia, adunque, posseva con le
forze sua assaltare Napoli, e' doveva farlo; se non poteva,
non doveva dividerlo. E se la divisione fece, con e'
Viniziani, di Lombardia, meritò scusa per avere con
quella messo el piè in Italia; questa merita biasimo, per
non essere escusata da quella necessità.

Aveva, dunque, Luigi fatto questi cinque errori: spenti
e minori potenti; acresciuto in Italia potenzia a uno potente; messo in quella uno forestiere potentissimo; non
venuto ad abitarvi; non vi messe colonie. E quali errori
ancora, vivendo lui, possevano non lo offendere, se non
avessi fatto el sesto: di torre lo stato a' Viniziani; perchè,
quando e' non avessi fatto grande la Chiesa nè messo in
Italia Spagna, era ben ragionevole e necessario abbassarli;
ma, avendo preso quelli primi partiti, non doveva mai
consentire alla ruina loro; perchè, sendo quelli potenti,
arebbono sempre tenuti gli altri discosto dalla impresa di
Lombardia, sì perchè e Viniziani non vi arebbono consen-
tito sanza diventarne signori loro, sì perchè gli altri non
arebbono voluto torla a Francia per darla a loro; e andare
a urtarli tutti e dua non arebbono avuto animo. E se alcuno dicesse: el re Luigi cedè ad Alessandro la Romagna
e a Spagna il Regno per fuggire una guerra, respondo con
le ragioni dette di sopra: che non si debbe mai lasciare

so that the ambitious and unhappy citizens of that province might have another to appeal to; and where he could have left a tributary king[17] in charge of that kingdom, he cast him out, putting one there who could, in turn, throw him out.

The desire to acquire is truly a very natural and common thing; and whenever men who can, do so, they are praised and not condemned; but when they cannot and want to do so just the same, herein lies the mistake and the condemnation. If France, then, with her own forces could have attacked Naples, she should have done so; if she could not, she should not have divided it. And if the division of Lombardy with the Venetians deserved to be excused in that it allowed Louis to get a foothold in Italy, the other division deserves to be condemned, for there is no excuse of necessity.

Louis, therefore, had made these five mistakes: he had extinguished the weaker powers; increased the power in Italy of a powerful force;[18] brought into that country a most powerful foreigner;[19] did not come to live in Italy; did not bring in colonies. Nevertheless, these mistakes, if he had lived, might not have hurt him if he had not made a sixth: that of depriving the Venetians of their power;[20] for if he had not made the Church powerful nor brought Spain into Italy, it would have been most sensible and necessary to put down the Venetians; but having taken those first steps, he never should have allowed them to be ruined; for while they remained powerful they always would have kept the others from attempting to take Lombardy, in part because the Venetians would not have allowed this unless they themselves were to become the rulers of Lombardy, and in part because the others would not have wanted to take it from France in order to give it to them, and they would not have had the

seguire uno disordine per fuggire una guerra; perchè la non si fugge, ma si differisce a tuo disavvantaggio. E se alcuni altri allegassero la fede che il re aveva obligata al papa, di fare per lui quella impresa per la resoluzione del suo matrimonio e il cappello di Roano; respondo con quello che per me di sotto si dirà circa la fede de' principi e come la si debbe osservare.

Ha perduto, adunque, el re Luigi la Lombardia per non avere osservato alcuno di quelli termini osservati da altri che hanno preso provincie e volutole tenere. Nè è miracolo alcuno questo, ma molto ordinario e ragionevole. E di questa materia parlai a Nantes con Roano, quando el Valentino (che così era chiamato popularmente Cesare Borgia, figliuolo di papa Alessandro) occupava la Romagna; perchè, dicendomi el cardinale di Roano che li Italiani non si intendevano della guerra, io li risposi che e Franzesi non si intendevano dello stato; perchè, se se ne intendessono, non lascerebbono venire la Chiesa in tanta grandezza. E per esperienza si è visto che la grandezza, in Italia, di quella e di Spagna è stata causata da Francia, e la ruina sua causata da loro. Di che si cava una regola generale, la quale mai o raro falla: che chi è cagione che uno diventi potente, ruina; perchè quella potenzia è causata da colui o con industria o con forza, e l'una e l'altra di queste due è sospetta a chi è diventato potente.

courage to provoke both of them. And if someone were to say: King Louis surrendered Romagna to Alexander and the kingdom of Naples to Spain in order to avoid going to war, I would answer with the arguments expressed above: that one must never permit disorder to develop in order to avoid going to war, because one does not avoid war but rather defers it to his own disadvantage. And if some others were to cite the promise that the King had made the Pope to undertake that enterprise in exchange for the annulment of his marriage[21] and the Cardinal's hat of Rouen,[22] I would answer with what I shall say further on concerning the promise of princes and how it should be observed.[23]

And so, King Louis lost Lombardy by not having observed any of the precepts observed by others who have taken over provinces and wished to hold on to them. Nor is this in any way a miracle, but very natural and reasonable. And I spoke about this matter with the Cardinal of Rouen at Nantes when Valentino (this was what Cesare Borgia, son of Pope Alexander, was commonly called) was occupying Romagna:[24] for the Cardinal of Rouen telling me that the Italians had no understanding of war, I answered that the French had no understanding of politics; because if they did understand, they would not allow the Church to gain so much power. And through experience we have seen that the power of the Church and of Spain in Italy has been brought about by France, and that her ruin has been caused by them. From this we extract a general rule which never or rarely fails: that whoever is the cause of another's coming into power ruins himself, because that power is brought about by him either through cleverness or force; and both the one and the other of these two are suspect to the one who has come into power.

NOTES

1. Chapter III picks up where the first paragraph of Chapter II leaves off.

2. The literal translation would be "strong medicines."

3. Louis XII, King of France from 1498–1515, laid claim to the duchy of Milan in 1499 as a descendant of the Visconti. He sent an army there commanded by Captain Gian Giacomo Trivulzio, who succeeded in occupying the duchy and expelling Ludovico il Moro, but because of the bad governing of the French oppressors, Milan soon rebelled.

4. Ludovico il Moro, son of Francesco Sforza, duke of Milan, recovered Milan on February 5, 1500, only to lose it again to the French in April of 1500. On this occasion he was betrayed by the Swiss mercenary soldiers he had hired, taken prisoner, and led into France, where he died ten years later.

5. "The whole world" refers to the Lega Santa, fostered by Julius II for the purpose of expelling the French from Italy. This coalition, organized in October 1511, consisted chiefly of the papacy, Ferdinand of Spain, and the Republic of Venice.

6. Burgundy became French in 1477; Brittany was acquired in 1491 as part of the dowry of Anne de Britagne, wife of Louis XII; Gascony was taken from the English in 1453; Normandy was annexed to France in 1204.

7. Greece here indicates the whole Balkan peninsula, the extension of the Byzantine Empire which had its capital at Constantinople, conquered by the Turks in 1453.

8. The League of Aetolia became an ally of the Romans in 211 B.C., aiding them in their war against Philip of Macedonia; the Aetolians then became dissatisfied with their share of the spoils and joined with Antiochus of Syria against their former allies, the Romans.

9. Antiochus was the king of Syria, defeated by the Romans at Magnesia (190 B.C.).

10. Charles VIII.

11. From September 1494 to October 1495.

12. Treaty of Blois, April 1499.

13. Charles' early successes in Italy alarmed Spain, the Empire, and many Italian princes, to the extent that they formed a coalition against him.

14. The Marquis of Mantua is Francesco Gonzaga; Duke of Ferrara is Ercole d'Este; Lady of Forlì, Catherine Riario Sforza;

Lord of Faenza, Astorre Manfredi; Lord of Pesaro, Giovanni Sforza; Lord of Rimini, Pandolfo Malatesta; Lord of Camerino, Giulio Cesare Varano; Lord of Piombino, Jacopo iv d'Appiano. All of these little "signori" were expelled from the State or were killed by Valentino in Tuscany between 1500 and 1502.

15. Alexander vi, a Borgia, had newly reaffirmed the secular power of the Church, and had initiated for the work of his son Cesare a policy of penetration and predominance in central Italy. Louis xii, having just joined with Milan, sent aids to Pope Borgia, increasing the latter's prestige, which was already so great, and reducing his own power by losing the Venetians (his friends), who were jealous of the Church.

16. Treaty of Granada (1500).

17. Frederick of Aragon.

18. Pope Alexander vi.

19. Ferdinand of Spain.

20. Pope Julius ii organized the League of Cambrai (1508) to enlist the help of France, Spain, and the Empire against the Venetians.

21. His marriage to Jeanne, daughter of Louis xi of France.

22. Because of this promise Louis xii's favorite, George d'Amboise, was made a cardinal by Alexander in 1498.

23. See Chapter xviii.

24. The conversation took place at the court of France during Machiavelli's diplomatic mission there in 1500.

IV Cur Darii Regnum Quod Alexander Occupaverat a Successoribus Suis Post Alexandri Mortem non Defecit

Considerate le difficultà quali si hanno a tenere uno stato di nuovo acquistato, potrebbe alcuno maravigliarsi donde nacque che Alessandro Magno diventò signore della Asia in pochi anni e, non l'avendo appena occupata, morì; donde pareva ragionevole che tutto quello stato si rebellassi; nondimeno e successori di Alessandro se lo mantenneno, e non ebbero, a tenerlo, altra difficultà che quella che intra loro medesimi, per ambizione propria, nacque. Respondo come e principati de' quali si ha memoria si truovano governati in dua modi diversi: o per uno principe e tutti gli altri servi, e quali come ministri, per grazia e concessione sua, aiutono governare quello regno; o per uno principe e per baroni, e quali, non per grazia del signore, ma per antiquità di sangue tengano quel grado. Questi tali baroni hanno stati e sudditi proprii, e quali li riconoscono per signori e hanno in loro naturale affezione. Quelli stati che si governano per uno principe e per servi, hanno el loro principe con più autorità; perchè in tutta la sua provincia non è alcuno che riconosca per superiore se non lui; e se obediscano alcuno altro, lo fanno come ministro e offiziale, e non li portano particulare amore.

Li esempli di queste dua diversità di governi sono, ne' nostri tempi, el Turco e il re di Francia. Tutta la monarchia del Turco è governata da uno signore; gli altri sono sua servi; e distinguendo il suo regno in Sangiachi, vi manda diversi amministratori, e gli muta e varia come pare a lui. Ma il re di Francia è posto in mezzo d'una moltitudine antiquata di signori, in quello stato riconosciuti da' loro sudditi e amati da quelli; hanno le loro preeminenzie; non le può il re torre loro sanza suo peri-

IV   Why the Kingdom of Darius, Which Was Occupied by Alexander, Did Not, After the Death of Alexander, Rebel Against His Successors

Bearing in mind the difficulties one encounters in holding on to a newly acquired state, one might wonder how it happened that when Alexander the Great,[1] having become ruler of Asia in a few years and scarcely having occupied it, died—whereby it would seem reasonable for the entire state to rebel—Alexander's successors, nevertheless, managed to keep possession of it; and they had, in holding on to it, no other difficulty than that which originated among themselves from their own ambitions.[2] Let me answer by saying that all those principalities we know about are governed in two different ways: either by a prince with all the rest as his servants, who, as ministers, through his kindness and permission, help govern that kingdom; or by a prince and barons, who, not because of any kindness on the part of the master, but because of noble lineage, hold that position. Such barons as these have their own states and subjects who acknowledge them as masters and are naturally fond of them. Those states governed by a prince and his servants hold their prince in greater authority, for in all his province there is no one that may be acknowledged as a superior if not himself; and if they do obey any others, they do so as his minister and official, for whom they bear no special love.

Examples of these two different kinds of governments in our own day are the Turk and the King of France. The entire Turkish empire is governed by one master; all the rest are his servants; and dividing his kingdom into provinces,[3] he sends various administrators there, and he moves and changes them around as he sees fit. But the King of France is situated among a group of long-established nobles, acknowledged in that state by their subjects and loved by them: they have their hereditary rights; the

culo. Chi considera, adunque, l'uno e l'altro di questi stati, troverrà difficultà nello acquistare lo stato del Turco, ma, vinto che sia, facilità grande a tenerlo. Così, per adverso, troverrete per qualche rispetto più facilità a occupare lo stato di Francia, ma difficultà grande a tenerlo.

Le cagioni della difficultà in potere occupare el regno del Turco, sono per non potere essere chiamato da' principi di quello regno, nè sperare, con la ribellione di quelli ch'egli ha d'intorno, potere facilitare la sua impresa. Il che nasce dalle ragioni sopradette; perchè, sendoli tutti stiavi e obligati, si possono con più difficultà corrompere; e quanda bene si corrompessero, se ne può sperare poco utile, non possendo quelli tirarsi drieto e populi per le ragioni assegnate. Onde chi asalta il Turco è necessario pensare di averlo a trovare tutto unito, e gli conviene sperare più nelle forze proprie che ne' disordini d'altri. Ma vinto che fussi, e rotto alla campagna in modo che non possa rifare eserciti, non si ha a dubitare di altro che del sangue del principe; il quale spento, non resta alcuno di chi si abbi a temere, non avendo gli altri credito con gli populi: e come el vincitore, avanti la vittoria, non poteva sperare in loro, così non debbe, dopo quella, temere di loro.

El contrario interviene ne' regni governati come quello di Francia; perchè con facilità tu puoi entrarvi, guadagnandoti alcuno barone del regno; perchè sempre si truova de' mal contenti e di quelli che desiderano innovare; costoro, per le ragioni dette, ti possono aprire la via a quello stato e facilitarti la vittoria. La quale di poi, a volerti mantenere, si tira drieto infinite difficultà e con quelli che ti hanno aiutato e con quelli che tu hai op-

King cannot retract them without endangering himself. Whoever studies, then, each of these two states, will find that the difficulty is in taking possession of the Turkish state, but once it has been conquered it is very easy to hold on to. And so, to the contrary, you will in some respects find that it is easier to occupy the French state, but it is very difficult to hold on to it.

The reasons for the difficulty in being able to occupy the Turkish kingdom are that it is not possible to be called there by the rulers of that kingdom nor to hope, with the rebellion of those the ruler has around him, to facilitate your undertaking. And this all stems from the reasons mentioned above: since they are all slaves and dependent, it is more difficult to corrupt them; and even if they were to be corrupted, one cannot hope they will be very useful, unable as they are to attract followers for the reasons already mentioned. Therefore, whoever assaults the Turks must expect to find them entirely united, and it is to his advantage to rely more on his own strength than on their disunity. But if the ruler of that state were to be beaten and broken in battle so that he could not reform his troops, there is nothing else to be feared except the family of the prince; once it is extinguished, there remains nobody else to be feared, for the others have no standing with the people; and just as the victor before the victory could not place hope in them, so now, afterward, he need not fear them.

The opposite takes place in kingdoms governed like France, because you can enter these with ease, once you have won over some baron of the kingdom; for one always finds some unhappy people as well as those who desire a change; these people, for the reasons already given, can open the way to that state and make the victory easy for you. Then, the desire to hold on to it is accompanied by endless difficulties with both those

pressi; nè ti basta spegnere el sangue del principe, perchè
vi rimangono quelli signori, che si fanno capi delle nuove
alterazioni; e non gli potendo nè contentare nè spegnere,
perdi quello stato qualunque volta venga la occasione.

Ora, se voi considerrete di qual natura di governi era
quello di Dario, lo troverrete simile al regno del Turco;
e però ad Alessandro fu necessario prima urtarlo tutto
e torli la campagna; dopo la quale vittoria, sendo Dario
morto, rimase ad Alessandro quello stato sicuro per le
ragioni di sopra discorse. E li suoi successori, se fussino
suti uniti, se lo potevano godere oziosi; nè in quel regno
nacquono altri tumulti che quelli che loro proprii susci-
torno. Ma gli stati ordinati come quello di Francia è
impossible possederli con tanta quiete. Di qui nacquono
le spesse rebellioni di Spagna, di Francia e di Grecia da'
Romani, per li spessi principati che erano in quelli stati;
de' quali mentre durò la memoria, sempre ne furono e
Romani incerti di quella possessione; ma spenta la memoria di quelli, con la potenzia e diuturnità dello imperio, ne diventorno securi possessori. E posserno anche,
quelli, combattendo di poi infra loro, ciascuno tirarsi
drieto parte di quelle provincie, secondo la autorità vi
aveva presa drento; e quelle, per essere el sangue de' loro
antiqui signori spento, non riconoscevano se non e Romani. Considerato, adunque, tutte queste cose, non si
maraviglierà alcuno della facilità ebbe Alessandro a tenere
lo stato di Asia, e delle difficultà che hanno avuto gli
altri a conservare lo acquistato, come Pirro e molti. Il che
non è nato dalla molta o poca virtù del vincitore, ma
dalla disformità del subietto.

who have aided you and those you have oppressed; nor is it enough to extinguish the family of the prince, because there remain those nobles who make themselves heads of the new reactionary factions; and able neither to make them happy nor to extinguish them, you lose that state as soon as the occasion presents itself.

Now, if you will consider the kind of government Darius[4] had, you will find it similar to the Turkish kingdom; and so Alexander first had to overthrow it completely and defeat them in battle;[5] after this victory, with Darius dead, that state remained securely in the possession of Alexander for the reasons discussed above. And his successors, had they been united, could have enjoyed it with ease; for in that kingdom no commotions arose other than those they themselves incited. But in regard to states organized like France, it is impossible to keep hold of them with as much ease. On this account there arose the frequent rebellions of Spain, France and Greece against the Romans, all due to the numerous principalities that existed in those states: as long as the memory of these endured, the Romans were always insecure in their possession; but once their memory was extinguished, with the strength and permanence of the empire, they became sure possessors. Then afterward, when the Romans began fighting among themselves, each one was able to attract a following from those provinces, depending on the authority he had there; and since the family line of their old ruler had been extinguished, they acknowledged only the Romans. Considering all these things, therefore, no one at all should marvel at the facility with which Alexander held on to the state of Asia, or at the difficulties that others have had in retaining their possession, such as Pyrrhus[6] and many others. This does not come about from greater or lesser ingenuity on the part of the victor, but rather from the disparity of the situations.

NOTES

1. Alexander the Great, King of Macedonia from 356–323 B.C. and son of Philip II, obtained regency of the kingdom when he was sixteen years old. In seven years he occupied all of Asia as far as India.

2. At his death, the Empire was divided among seven generals. The struggles that rose among them upset the Empire, and the enormous dominion finally broke up into eleven kingdoms.

3. This word is probably of Turkish origin, and its original meaning is "flag" or "banner."

4. Darius III was the king of Persia (337–330 B.C.), who in four years lost his empire to Alexander the Great.

5. "Torlì la campagna" is an expression that refers to a specific type of defeat in which the losing party is forced to retreat to some fortress.

6. Pyrrhus, King of Epirus (319–272 B.C.), conquered southern Italy and Sicily in a very short time.

V Quomodo Administrandae Sunt Civitates vel Principatus, Qui Antequam Occuparentur Suis Legibus Vivebant

Quando quelli stati che si acquistono, come è detto, sono consueti a vivere con le loro legge e in libertà, a volerli tenere ci sono tre modi: el primo, ruinarle; l' altro, andarvi ad abitare personalmente; el terzo, lasciarle vivere con le sua legge, traendone una pensione e creandovi drento uno stato di pochi che te le conservino amiche. Perchè, sendo quello stato creato da quello principe, sa che non può stare sanza la amicizia e potenzia sua, e ha a fare tutto per mantenerlo; e più facilmente si tiene una città usa a vivere libera con il mezzo de' sua cittadini, che in alcuno altro modo, volendola preservare.

In exemplis ci sono li Spartani e li Romani. Li Spartani tenneno Atene e Tebe creandovi uno stato di pochi; tamen le riperderno. Li Romani, per tenere Capua, Cartagine e Numanzia, le disfeciono; e non le perderno; vollono tenere la Grecia quasi come tenneno li Spartani, faccendola libera e lasciandoli le sue leggi, e non successe loro; in modo che furono costretti disfare di molte città di quella provincia, per tenerla. Perchè, in verità, non ci è modo nessuno secure a possederle, altro che la ruina. E chi diviene patrone di una città consueta a vivere libera, e non la disfacci, aspetti di essere disfatto da quella; perchè sempre ha per refugio, nella rebellione, el nome della libertà e gli ordini antiqui suoi, e quali nè per la lunghezza de' tempi nè per benefizii mai si dimenticano. E per cosa che si faccia o si provegga, se non si disuniscono o dissipano gli abitatori, e' non sdimenticano quel nome nè quelli ordini; e subito, in ogni accidente, vi ricorrono; come fe' Pisa dopo cento anni che l' era suta posta in servitù da' Fiorentini. Ma quando le città o le provincie

V How Cities or Principalities That Lived by Their Own Laws Before They Were Occupied Should Be Governed

When those states that are acquired, as I have said,[1] are accustomed to living by their own laws and in freedom, there are three ways to hold on to them: the first, to demolish them; the second, to go there in person to live; the third, to let them live by their own laws, obliging them to pay tribute and establishing therein a government consisting of a few people who will keep the state friendly toward you. For that government, having been created by that prince, knows that it cannot survive without his friendship and power, and it must do all possible to maintain them; and a city used to living in freedom is more easily held by means of its own citizens than in any other way, if you chose to preserve it.[2]

As examples there are the Spartans and the Romans. The Spartans held Athens and Thebes by establishing therein a government consisting of a few people, though eventually they lost both of them. The Romans, to hold on to Capua, Carthage and Numantia, destroyed them, and did not lose them; they wanted to keep Greece in almost the same way the Spartans kept it, making it free and leaving it with its own laws, and they did not succeed; so they were forced to destroy many of the cities in that province in order to hold on to it. For the truth is that there is no sure way of keeping possession of them, except by demolishing them. And whoever becomes master of a city accustomed to living in freedom and does not destroy it may expect to be destroyed by it; because this city can always have refuge, during a rebellion, in the name of liberty and its traditional institutions, neither of which, either with the passing of time or the acquiring of benefits, are ever forgotten. And no matter what one does or provides for, if one does not disunite or dis-

sono use a vivere sotto uno principe, e quel sangue sia spento, sendo da uno canto usi ad obedire, dall' altro non avendo el principe vecchio, farne uno infra loro non si accordono, vivere liberi non sanno; di modo che sono più tardi a pigliare le armi, e con più facilità se li può uno principe guadagnare e assicurarsi di loro. Ma nelle republichè maggiore vita, maggiore odio, più desiderio di vendetta; nè li lascia, nè può lasciare riposare la memoria della antiqua libertà; tale che la più secura via è spegnerle o abitarvi.

perse the inhabitants of such a city, they will not forget that name or those institutions, and immediately, in every case, they will resort to them, just as Pisa did after the hundred years that it had been held in servitude by the Florentines.[3] But when cities or provinces are used to living under a prince, and the family line of that prince has been extinguished, being on the one hand used to obeying while on the other not having their old prince, and not able to agree on a choice of one from among themselves, yet not knowing how to live in freedom, they are, as a result, slower in taking up arms, and a prince can, with greater ease, win them over and find security in them. But in the case of republics there is greater life, greater hatred, more desire for revenge; the memory of their ancient liberty will not and cannot allow them to rest; so that the surest way is to destroy them or take up residence there.

NOTES

1. Referring in particular to Chapter III.

2. As opposed to destroying it, which is the first way.

3. Actually, Pisa was ruled by Florence for 88 years (1405–1494) and not one hundred—an example, though slight, of Machiavelli's frequent distortion of historical fact.

VI   De Principatibus Novis Qui Armis Propriis et Virtute Acquiruntur

Non si maravigli alcuno se nel parlare che io farò de' principati al tutto nuovi e di principe e di stato, io addurrò grandissimi esempli; perchè, camminando gli uomini quasi sempre per le vie battute da altri, e procedendo nelle azioni loro con le imitazioni, nè si potendo le vie di altri al tutto tenere nè alla virtù di quelli che tu imiti aggiugnere, debbe uno uomo prudente entrare sempre per vie battute da uomini grandi, e quelli che sono stati eccellentissimi imitare, acciò che, se la sua virtù non vi arriva, almeno ne renda qualche odore; e fare come gli arcieri prudenti, a' quali, parendo el loco dove disegnano ferire troppo lontano, e conoscendo fino a quanto va la virtù del loro arco, pongono la mira assai più alta che il loco destinato, non per aggiugnere con la loro freccia a tanta altezza, ma per potere, con lo aiuto di sì alta mira, pervenire al disegno loro.

Dico, adunque, che ne' principati tutti nuovi, dove sia uno nuovo principe, si truova, a mantenerli, più o meno difficultà, secondo che più o meno è virtuoso colui che gli acquista. E perchè questo evento di diventare, di privato, principe, presuppone o virtù o fortuna, pare che l' una o l' altra di queste dua cose mitighi, in parte, di molte difficultà; nondimanco, colui che è stato meno in su la fortuna, si è mantenuto più. Genera ancora facilità essere il principe costretto, per non avere altri stati, venire personalmente ad abitarvi. Ma per venire a quelli che per propria virtù, e non per fortuna, sono diventati principi, dico che li più eccellenti sono Moisè, Ciro, Romulo, Teseo e simili. E benchè di Moisè non si debba ragionare, sendo suto uno mero esecutore delle cose che li erano ordinate da Dio, tamen debbe essere ammirato solum per quella grazia che lo faceva degno di parlare con Dio. Ma consideriamo Ciro

VI On New Principalities Acquired by Means of One's Own Arms and Ingenuity

No one should be surprised if, in my discussion of principalities that are completely new in respect to their prince and composition, I make use of the most outstanding examples; since men almost always walk the path made by others and conduct their affairs through imitation, although they are not altogether able to stay on the path of others nor arrive at the ingenuity of those they imitate, a prudent man should always take the path trodden by great men and imitate those who have been most outstanding;[1] so that, if his own ingenuity does not come up to theirs, at least it will have the smell of it; and he should act like those prudent archers, who, when the target they are aiming at seems too far off, aware of the capacity of their bow, set their sight a good deal higher than the desired target, not to reach such a height with their arrow but rather to be able, with the help of aiming high, to reach their target.

I say, then, that in entirely new principalities, where there is a new prince, one will find more or less difficulty in maintaining them according to the greater or lesser ingenuity of the one who acquires them. And since this event of transition from ordinary citizen to prince presupposes either ingenuity or fortune, it would seem that either the one or the other of these two things should, to some extent, mitigate many of the difficulties; nevertheless, he who has trusted less in fortune has held on to his position best. Things are made easier also by the fact that the prince, having no other state to rule, is forced to come and live there in person. But to come to those who, by means of their own ingenuity and not by fortune, have become princes, let me say that the most outstanding are Moses, Cyrus, Romulus, Theseus and the like. And although one should not discuss Moses, for he was a

e li altri che hanno acquistato o fondato regni: li troverrete tutti mirabili; e se si considerranno le azioni e ordini
loro particulari, parranno non discrepanti da quelli di
Moisè, che ebbe sì gran precettore. Ed esaminando le
azioni e vita loro, non si vede che quelli avessero altro
dalla fortuna che la occasione; la quale dette loro materia
a potere introdurvi drento quella forma parse loro; e sanza
quella occasione la virtù dello animo loro si sarebbe
spenta, e sanza quella virtù la occasione sarebbe venuta
invano.

Era dunque necessario a Moisè trovare il populo d' Isdrael, in Egitto, stiavo e oppresso dalli Egizii, acciò che
quelli, per uscire di servitù, si disponessino a sequirlo.
Conveniva che Romulo non capissi in Alba, fussi stato
esposto al nascere, a volere che diventassi re di Roma e
fondatore di quella patria. Bisognava che Ciro trovassi e
Persi mal contenti dello imperio de' Medi, e li Medi molli
ed effeminati per la lunga pace. Non posseva Teseo dimostrare la sua virtù, se non trovava li Ateniesi dispersi.
Queste occasioni, pertanto, fecioro questi uomini felici,
e la eccellente virtù loro fece quella occasione essere conosciuta; donde la loro patria ne fu nobilitata e diventò
felicissima.

Quelli e quali per vie virtuose, simili a costoro, diventano principi, acquistono el principato con difficultà, ma
con facilità lo tengono; e le difficultà che gli hanno nello
acquistare el principato, in parte nascono da' nuovi ordini
e modi che sono forzati introdurre per fondare lo stato
loro e la loro securtà. E debbasi considerare come e' non
è cosa più difficile a trattare, nè più dubbia a riuscire, nè

mere executor of the things God had commanded, he still should be admired if only for that grace which made him worthy of speaking with God.[2] But let us consider Cyrus[3] and the others who acquired or founded kingdoms: you will find them all admirable; and if their particular actions and institutions are examined, they do not appear to differ from those of Moses, who had so great a preceptor. And examining their actions and lives, we see that from fortune they received nothing but the occasion; which in turn offered them the material they could then shape into whatever form they pleased; and without that occasion their very ingenuity would have been extinguished, and without that ingenuity the occasion would have come in vain.

Therefore it was necessary for Moses to find the people of Israel in Egypt slaves and oppressed by the Egyptians, so that they, in order to escape this servitude, might be disposed to following him. It was imperative that Romulus[4] not remain in Alba and for him to be exposed at birth, so that he might become king of Rome and founder of that nation. It was requisite that Cyrus find the Persians dissatisfied with the empire of the Medes and the Medes soft and effeminate through years of peace. Theseus[5] could not have displayed his ingenuity if he had not found the Athenians dispersed. These occasions, then, made these men successful, and their outstanding ingenuity made that occasion known to them; whereby their nations were made renowned and they became prosperous.

Those who, like these men, become princes by means of ingenuity, acquire their principality with difficulty, but hold on to it with ease; and the difficulties they encounter in acquiring the principality arise, in part, from the new institutions and methods they are forced to introduce in order to establish their state and their security. And it should be kept in mind that there is nothing more diffi-

più periculosa a maneggiare, che farsi capo a introdurre nuovi ordini; perchè lo introduttore ha per nimici tutti quelli chi delli ordini vecchi fanno bene, e ha tepidi defensori tutti quelli che delli ordini nuovi farebbono bene. La quale tepidezza nasce, parte per paura delli avversarii, che hanno le leggi dal canto loro, parte dalla incredulità delli uomini; e quali non credano in verità le cose nuove, se non ne veggano nata una ferma esperienzia; donde nasce che, qualunche volta quelli che sono nimici hanno occasione di assaltare, lo fanno partigianamente, e quelli altri defendano tepidamente; in modo che insieme con loro si periclita.

È necessario pertanto, volendo discorrere bene questa parte, esaminare se questi innovatori stanno per loro medesimi, o se dependano da altri: cioè, se per condurre l'opera loro bisogna che preghino, o vero possono forzare. Nel primo caso capitano sempre male e non conducano cosa alcuna; ma quando dependano da loro proprii e possono forzare, allora è che rare volte periclitano. Di qui nacque che tutti e profeti armati vinsono, e gli disarmati ruinorno. Perchè, oltra alle cose dette, la natura de' populi è varia; ed è facile a persuadere loro una cosa, ma è difficile fermarli in quella persuasione; e però conviene essere ordinato in modo che, quando e' non credano più, si possa fare credere loro per forza. Moisè, Ciro, Teseo e Romulo non arebbono possuto fare osservare loro lungamente le loro costituzioni, se fussino stati disarmati; come ne' nostri tempi intervenne a fra' Ieronimo Savonarola, il quale ruinò ne' sua ordini nuovi, come la moltitudine cominciò a non crederli; e lui non aveva modo a potere tenere fermi quelli che avevano creduto, nè a far credere e discredenti. Però questi tali hanno nel condursi gran difficultà, e tutti e loro periculi sono fra via, e conviene che con la virtù gli superino; ma superati che gli hanno, e che cominciano

cult to carry out nor more doubtful of success nor more dangerous to manage than to introduce a new system of things; for the introducer has as his enemies all those who benefit from the old system, and lukewarm defenders in all those who would benefit from by the new system. This lukewarmness originates partly from fear of their adversaries, who have the law on their side, and partly from the incredulousness of men in general, who do not really believe something new unless they actually have had experience with it; therefore it happens that, whenever those who are enemies have the occasion to attack, they do so with the fervor of partisans, and those others come to the defense lukewarmly, so that both the prince and his friends are in danger.

It is necessary, however, if we wish to discuss this matter thoroughly, to observe whether these innovators stand on their own or are dependent on others; that is, if in order to carry out their work, they are obliged to beg, or are able to use force. In the first case, they always come to a bad end and never achieve anything; but when they depend on themselves and are able to use force, then very seldom will they find themselves in danger. From this comes the fact that the armed prophets conquered and the unarmed came to ruin. Besides what has been said, people in general are unstable; and it is easy to persuade them of something but difficult to hold them to that persuasion; and therefore things should be arranged so that, when people no longer believe, they can be made to believe by force. Had Moses, Cyrus, Theseus and Romulus been unarmed they would not have had their institutions respected by the people for very long; just as in our own times it happened to Brother Girolamo Savonarola,[6] who was defeated by his new institutions when the multitude began not to believe in him; and he had no means of holding firm those who had believed nor of making the disbelievers believe. Therefore men such as these have

ad essere in venerazione, avendo spenti quelli che di sua qualità gli avevano invidia, rimangono potenti, securi, onorati, felici.

A sì alti esempli io voglio aggiugnere uno esemplo minore; ma bene arà qualche proporzione con quelli, e voglio mi basti per tutti li altri simili; e questo è Ierone Siracusano. Costui di privato diventò principe di Siracusa; nè ancora lui conobbe altro dalla fortuna che la occasione; perchè, sendo e Siracusani oppressi, lo elessero per loro capitano; donde meritò di essere fatto loro principe. E fu di tanta virtù, etiam in privata fortuna, che chi ne scrive dice «quod nihil illi deerat ad regnandum praeter regnum». Costui spense la milizia vecchia, ordinò della nuova; lasciò le amicizie antiche, prese delle nuove; e come ebbe amicizie e soldati che fussino sua, possè in su tale fondamento edificare ogni edifizio; tanto che lui durò assai fatica in acquistare e poca in mantenere.

NOTES

1. Here is introduced one of the author's basic themes: the imitation of great men, which, according to Machiavelli, is natural to man and shapes history.

2. Perhaps Machiavelli is speaking ironically here.

3. Cyrus (599–529 B.C.) was the founder of the Persian Empire (560 B.C.).

4. Romulus was the legendary founder of Rome (735 B.C.).

5. Theseus was the King of Athens and a major hero in Greek mythology.

6. Girolamo Savonarola, born in Ferrara in 1452, was a Dominican friar who came to Florence in 1481, where he succeeded in exciting the masses with his fantastic animated

great difficulty in getting ahead, and they encounter all their dangers as they advance, and they must overcome them by means of their ingenuity; but once they have overcome them and have begun to be held in veneration, and once they have done away with those who were envious of their abilities, they remain powerful, secure, honored, prosperous.[7]

To such lofty examples I wish to add a minor one that will, nevertheless, in some respect compare well to the others, and I want it to represent all similar cases: it is the example of Hiero of Syracuse.[8] From an ordinary citizen he became Prince of Syracuse; he too received nothing from fortune other than the occasion; for the citizens of Syracuse being oppressed, they chose him as their captain; and from that rank he proved himself worthy of becoming their prince. And he possessed so much ingenuity that, while still in private life, someone who wrote about him said "that he lacked nothing to be able to reign except a kingdom." He did away with the old militia, formed a new one; he put aside old alliances, made new ones; and once he had alliances and soldiers that were his own, he was able on such a foundation to build whatever building he pleased: so that it cost him great effort to acquire and little to maintain.

preaching. He ruled the Florentine republic with Soderini from 1494 (when Piero de' Medici was driven out). Opposed by the Pope, the nobility, the supporters of the Medici, and the Franciscans, he was hanged and burned in the Piazza della Signoria on May 23, 1498.

7. Notice the order of these words: because they are "powerful" they are "secure," etc.

8. Hiero ii (of Syracuse), the tyrant of Syracuse (263–214 B.C.), fought with Pyrrhus against the Carthaginians and then united with them to fight the Romans in the First Punic War. Then, recognizing the power of Rome, he became her ally for the duration of his reign.

VII De Principatibus Novis Qui Alienis Armis et Fortuna Acquiruntur

Coloro e quali solamente per fortuna diventano, di privati, principi, con poca fatica diventano, ma con assai si mantengano; e non hanno alcuna difficultà fra via, perchè vi volano; ma tutte le difficultà nascono quando e' sono posti. E questi tali sono, quando è concesso ad alcuno uno stato o per danari o per grazia di chi lo concede: • come intervenne a molti in Grecia, nelle città di Ionia e di Ellesponto, dove furono fatti principi da Dario, acciò le tenessino per sua securtà e gloria; come erano fatti ancora quelli imperadori che, di privati, per corruzione de' soldati, pervenivano allo imperio. Questi stanno semplicemente in su la volontà e fortuna di chi lo ha concesso loro, che sono dua cose volubilissime e instabili; e non sanno e non possono tenere quel grado: non sanno, perchè, se non è uomo di grande ingegno e virtù, non è ragionevole che, sendo sempre vissuto in privata fortuna, sappi comandare; non possono, perchè non hanno forze che gli possino essere amiche e fedeli. Di poi, li stati che vengano subito, come tutte le altre cose della natura che nascono e crescono presto, non possono avere le barbe e corrispondenzie loro; in modo che el primo tempo avverso le spenge; se già quelli tali, come è detto, che sì de repente sono diventati principi, non sono di tanta virtù, che quello che la fortuna ha messo loro in grembo e' sappino subito prepararsi a conservarlo, e quelli fondamenti che gli altri hanno fatti avanti che diventino principi, gli faccino poi.

Io voglio all'uno e all'altro di questi modi detti, circa el diventare principe per virtù o per fortuna, addurre dua esempli stati ne' dì della memoria nostra: e questi sono

VII On New Principalities Acquired with the Arms and Fortunes of Others

Those private citizens who through fortune alone become princes become so with little strain, but it requires a great deal for them to maintain their standing; they encounter no difficulties along the way because they soar to their position; rather all the difficulties arise when they have arrived. These are the men who are given a state because they possess money or the favor of the one who bestows it: as happened to many men in Greece, in the cities of Ionia and the Hellespont, where they were made princes by Darius[1] with the purpose of retaining these cities for his own security and glory; just as those emperors[2] who, from their position as private citizens, came to reign by corrupting the soldiers. These men depend simply upon two very volatile and unstable things, the will and fortune of the one who gave them the state; and they do not know how nor are they able to maintain their position. They do not know how because, unless they are men of great talent and ingenuity, it is not reasonable that, having always lived a private life, they know how to rule; they are not able because they could not have the kind of troops that are friendly and faithful. Moreover, states that are formed quickly, just as all other things in nature that spring up and grow rapidly, do not have roots and ramifications, so that the first bad weather destroys them, unless these men I have mentioned, who have suddenly become princes, are of such ingenuity that they can quickly prepare themselves and preserve what fortune has placed in their laps, and construct later those same foundations which others have constructed before becoming princes.

Concerning the two ways just mentioned of becoming a prince, by ingenuity or by fortune, I want to draw upon two examples that are of our times: they are Francesco

Francesco Sforza e Cesare Borgia. Francesco, per li debiti mezzi e con una grande sua virtù, di privato diventò duca di Milano; e quello che con mille affanni aveva acquistato, con poca fatica mantenne. Dall'altra parte Cesare Borgia, chiamato dal vulgo duca Valentino, acquistò lo stato con la fortuna del padre, e con quella lo perdè: nonostante che per lui si usassi ogni opera e facessi tutte quelle cose che per uno prudente e virtuoso uomo si dovea fare, per mettere le barbe sua in quelli stati che l'arme e fortuna d'altri gli aveva concessi. Perchè, come di sopra si disse, chi non fa e fondamenti prima, li potrebbe con una gran virtù farli poi, ancora che si faccino con disagio dello architettore e periculo dello edifizio. Se, adunque, si considerrà tutti e progressi del duca, si vedrà lui aversi fatti gran fondamenti alla futura potenzia; e quali non iudico superfluo discorrere, perchè io non saprei quali precetti mi dare migliori a uno principe nuovo, che lo esemplo delle azioni sua: e se li ordini suoi non gli profittorno, non fu sua colpa, perchè nacque da una estraordinaria ed estrema malignità di fortuna.

Aveva Alessandro vi, nel volere fare grande el duca suo figliuolo, assai difficultà presenti e future. Prima, e' non vedeva via di poterlo fare signore di alcuno stato che non fussi stato di Chiesa; e volgendosi a torre quello della Chiesa, sapeva che el duca di Milano e gli Viniziani non gnene consentirebbano; perchè Faenza e Rimino erano di già sotto la protezione de' Viniziani. Vedeva, oltre di questo, l'arme di Italia, e quelle in spezie di chi si fussi possuto servire, essere in le mani di coloro che dovevano temere la grandezza del papa; e però non se ne poteva fidare, sendo tutte nelli Orsini e Colonnesi e loro complici. Era, adunque, necessario che si turbassino quelli ordini, e disordinare li stati di coloro, per potersi insi-

Sforza[3] and Cesare Borgia.[4] Francesco, with the proper means and great ingenuity, from his position as a private citizen became Duke of Milan, and that which he acquired with countless hardships, he maintained with scarcely any trouble. On the other hand, Cesare Borgia, commonly called Duke Valentino,[5] acquired the state through the good fortune of his father, and by that same means he lost it; despite the fact that he used every means and did everything that a prudent and competent man should do in order to root himself firmly in those states that the arms and fortune of others had bestowed. For, as mentioned above, whoever does not first lay his foundations could, with great ingenuity, do so later, but always at the risk of the architect and the danger of the building. If, then, we study all the movements of the Duke, we will see that he laid strong foundations for his future power; I do not consider it superfluous to discuss them for I would not know of any better precept to give a new prince than the example of his actions; and if he did not profit from his methods, it was not his own fault but rather the result of an extraordinary and extreme maliciousness on the part of fortune.

Alexander VI, in his concern for the advancement of his son, the Duke, had many difficulties, both present and future. First, he saw no way of making him master of any state that did not already belong to the Church; and he knew that the Duke of Milan[6] and the Venetians would not consent to a move on his part to take anything belonging to the Church, because Faenza and Rimini were already under the protection of the Venetians. Besides this, he saw that Italy's troops, and in particular those he might have been able to utilize, were in the hands of those who had reason to fear the power of the Pope; and he could not rely on them, since they were all under the control of the Orsini and Colonna[7] and their followers.

gnorire securamente di parte di quelli. Il che li fu facile, perchè e' trovò e Viniziani che, mossi da altre cagioni, si erono volti a fare ripassare e Franzesi in Italia; il che non solamente non contradisse, ma lo fe' più facile con la resoluzione del matrimonio antiquo del re Luigi. Passò, adunque, il re in Italia con lo aiuto de' Viniziani e consenso di Alessandro; nè prima fu in Milano, che il papa ebbe da lui gente per la impresa di Romagna; la quale li fu consentita per la reputazione del re.

Acquistata, adunque, el duca la Romagna, e sbattuti e Colonnesi, volendo mantenere quella e procedere più avanti, lo impedivano dua cose: l' una, l' arme sua che non gli parevano fedeli, l' altra, la volontà di Francia: cioè che l' arme Orsine, delle quali s' era valuto, li mancassino sotto, e non solamente li impedissino lo acquistare, ma li togliessino lo acquistato; e che il re ancora non gli facessi el simile. Delli Orsini ne ebbe uno riscontro quando, dopo la espugnazione di Faenza, assaltò Bologna, chè gli vidde andare freddi in quello asalto; e, circa el re, conobbe l' animo suo quando, preso el ducato di Urbino, assaltò la Toscana; dalla quale impresa el re lo fece desistere. Onde che il duca deliberò non dependere più dalle arme e fortuna d' altri. E, la prima cosa, indebolì le parti Orsine e Colonnese in Roma; perchè tutti gli aderenti loro che fussino gentili uomini, se li guadagnò, faccendoli suoi gentili uomini e dando loro grandi provvisioni, e onorolli, secondo le loro qualità, di condotte e di governi; in modo che in pochi mesi nelli animi loro l' affezione delle parti si spense, e tutta si volse nel duca. Dopo questa, aspettò la occasione di spegnere e capi Orsini, avendo dispersi quelli di casa Colonna; la quale li venne bene, e lui la usò meglio; perchè, avvedutisi li Orsini,

Therefore, he had to upset this order of things and cause disorder among their states to be able to seize a firm control over a part of them. And this was easy for him to do, for he found that the Venetians, considering other reasons, were impelled to allow the French to come into Italy; not only did he not oppose this coming but he facilitated it with the annulment of King Louis' first marriage. The King, therefore, came into Italy with the aid of the Venetians and the consent of Alexander; no sooner had he reached Milan than the Pope got soldiers from him for the campaign in Romagna; they were given to him because of the King's reputation.

Then, having conquered the Romagna and vanquished the Colonna, the Duke, desiring to maintain his conquest and to continue further, was hindered by two things: one was that his troops did not seem faithful, the other was the will of France; that is to say, the troops of the Orsini, which he had been using, might betray him and impede not only his acquiring more, but might take away what he had already conquered, and the King, too, might do the same. He had one confirming experience with the Orsini troops when, after the battle of Faenza, he attacked Bologna and saw them go into battle without enthusiasm; in regard to the King, he came to know his mind, when, after the Duchy of Urbino was captured, he invaded Tuscany: the King made him give up that campaign.[8] Whereby the Duke decided no longer to depend upon the troops and fortune of others. And the first thing he did was to weaken the Orsini and Colonna factions in Rome; for he persuaded to his side all their followers who were noblemen, and made them his own noblemen and gave them large stipends; and he honored them with military and political appointments according to their qualifications; the result was that in just a few months their affection for the factions died out in their minds,

tardi, che la grandezza del duca e della Chiesa era la loro ruina, feciono una dieta alla Magione, nel Perugino; da quella nacque la rebellione di Urbino e li tumulti di Romagna e infiniti periculi del duca; e quali tutti superò con lo aiuto de' Franzesi. E ritornatogli la reputazione, nè si fidando di Francia nè di altre forze esterne, per non le avere a cimentare, si volse alli inganni; e seppe tanto dissimulare l' animo suo, che gli Orsini medesimi, mediante el signor Paulo, si riconciliorno seco; con il quale el duca non mancò d' ogni ragione di offizio per assicurarlo, dandogli danari, veste e cavalli; tanto che la simplicità loro li condusse a Sinigaglia nelle sua mani. Spenti, adunque, questi capi, e ridotti e partigiani loro sua amici, aveva il duca gittati assai buoni fondamenti alla potenzia sua, avendo tutta la Romagna con el ducato di Urbino, parendoli, massime, aversi acquistata amica la Romagna e guadagntosi tutti quelli popoli, per avere cominciato a gustare il bene essere loro.

E perchè questa parte è degna di notizia e da essere imitata da altri, non la voglio lasciare indrieto. Preso che ebbe il duca la Romagna, e trovandola suta comandata da signori impotenti, e quali più presto avevano spogliato e loro sudditi che corretti, e dato loro materia di disunione, non di unione, tanto che quella provincia era tutta piena di latrocinii, di brighe e di ogni altra ragione di insolenzia, iudicò fussi necessario, a volerla ridurre pacifica e obediente al braccio regio, darli buon governo.

and all of it was turned toward the Duke. After this he waited for the occasion to extinguish the Orsini family, having already dispersed the Colonna household; a good occasion arose, and the use he made of it was even better; for, when the Orsini realized, later, that the greatness of the Duke and the Church meant their ruin, they called for a conference at Magione[9] in the district of Perugia. From this gathering came the rebellion of Urbino and the uprising in Romagna and endless dangers for the Duke, all of which he overcame with the help of the French. And once he had regained his reputation, placing trust neither in France nor in other outside forces, so as not to take recourse in either of them, he turned to methods of deceit. And he knew how to disguise his intentions so well that the Orsini, represented by Signor Paulo, made peace with him; and the Duke did not fail to employ all kinds of courtesy to reassure Paulo, giving him money, clothes and horses; so that the simple-mindedness of the Orsini brought them to Sinigaglia[10] and into his hands. Having finished off these leaders and forced their followers into his friendship, the Duke had laid very good foundations for his power, possessing all of Romagna together with the Duchy of Urbino, and, more important, it seemed that he had acquired the friendship of Romagna and won over all of its population as soon as they began to get a taste of the good effects of his reign.

And since this point is worth understanding and being imitated by others, I do not want to pass over it. The Duke, having taken Romagna as he did and having found it ruled by powerless noblemen who had been quicker to despoil their subjects than to govern them, and gave them cause to disunite rather than to unite, so that the province was completely full of rapine, factions and all other kinds of dissension, he decided it was necessary, in order to bring peace and obedience of the law, to give

Però vi prepose messer Remirro de Orco, uomo crudele ed espedito, al quale dette pienissima potestà. Costui in poco tempo la ridusse pacifica e unita, con grandissima reputazione. Di poi iudicò el duca non essere necessario sì eccessiva autorità, perchè dubitava non divenissi odiosa; e preposevi uno iudicio civile nel mezzo della provincia, con uno presidente eccellentissimo, dove ogni città vi aveva lo avvocato suo. E perchè conosceva le rigorosità passate averli generato qualche odio, per purgare gli animi di quelli populi e quadagnarseli in tutto, volle mostrare che, se crudeltà alcuna era seguita, non era nata da lui, ma dalla acerba natura del ministro. E presa sopra questo occasione, lo fece a Cesena, una mattina, mettere in dua pezzi in su la piazza, con uno pezzo di legno e uno coltello sanguinoso a canto. La ferocità del quale spettaculo fece quelli populi in uno tempo rimanere satisfatti e stupidi.

Ma torniamo donde noi partimmo. Dico che, trovandosi el duca assai potente e in parte assicurato de' presenti periculi, per essersi armato a suo modo e avere in buona parte spente quelle arme che, vicine, lo potevano offendere, gli restava, volendo procedere con lo acquisto, il respetto del re di Francia; perchè conosceva come dal re, il quale tardi si era accorto dello errore suo, non li sarebbe sopportato. E cominciò, per questo, a cercare di amicizie nuove e vacillare con Francia, nella venuta che fecionogli Franzesi verso el regno di Napoli contro alli Spagnuoli che assediavono Gaeta. E lo animo suo era assicurarsi di loro; il che li sarebbe presto riuscito, se Alessandro viveva.

them the right kind of government. Therefore, he placed there Messer Remirro de Orca,[11] a cruel and efficient man, and put him in full charge. This man in a short time made the province peaceful and united, and in so doing made a great reputation for himself. Later, the Duke decided that such excessive authority was no longer necessary, for he feared that it might become odious; and in the middle of the province he established a civil court, with a very prominent president, in which every city was represented by its own lawyer. And since he knew that the severities of the past had brought about a certain amount of hate, in order to purge the minds of those people and win them over completely, he planned to demonstrate that if cruelty of any kind had come about, it did not stem from him but rather from the bitter nature of the minister. And having found the occasion to do this, he had him placed one morning in Cesena on the piazza in two pieces with a piece of wood and a bloodstained knife alongside him. The atrocity of such a spectacle left those people at one and the same time satisfied and stupefied.

But let us return to our theme. Let me say that the Duke, finding himself very powerful and in part secure from immediate dangers, having armed himself with his own troops and having to a large extent destroyed those neighboring forces[12] that might have harmed him, still had his relationship with the King of France to consider if he wished to go on with his conquest; for he knew that the King, who had recently become aware of his error, would not help him. Because of this he began to search for new alliances and to temporize with France during the expedition the French made to the Kingdom of Naples against the Spanish who were besieging Gaeta. And his mind was set upon assuring his position through

E questi furono e governi sua quanto alle cose presenti. Ma quanto alle future, lui aveva a dubitare, in prima, che uno nuovo successore alla Chiesa non li fussi amico e cercassi torli quello che Alessandro gli aveva dato. Di che pensò assicurarsi in quattro modi: prima, di spegnere tutti e sangui di quelli signori che lui aveva spogliati, per torre al papa quella occasione; secondo, di guadagnarsi tutti e gentili uomini di Roma, come è detto, per potere con quelli tenere el papa in freno; terzo, ridurre el Collegio più suo che poteva; quarto, acquistare tanto imperio, avanti che il papa morissi, che potessi per se medesimo resistere a uno primo impeto. Di queste quattro cose, alla morte di Alessandro ne aveva condotte tre; la quarta aveva quasi per condotta; perchè de' signori spogliati ne ammazzò quanti ne possè aggiugnere, e pochissimi si salvorno; e gentili uomini romani si aveva guadagnati, e nel Collegio aveva grandissima parte; e quanto al nuovo acquisto, aveva disegnato diventare signore di Toscana, e possedeva di già Perugia e Piombino, e di Pisa aveva presa la protezione. E come non avessi avuto ad avere respetto a Francia (chè non gliene aveva ad avere più, per essere di già e Franzesi spogliati del Regno dalli Spagnoli, di qualità che ciascuno di loro era necessitato comperare l'amicizia sua) e' saltava in Pisa. Dopo questo, Lucca e Siena cedeva subito, parte per invidia de' Fiorentini, parte per paura; e Fiorentini non avevano remedio. Il che se gli fussi riuscito (che gli riusciva l'anno medesimo che Alessandro morì) si acquistava tante forze e tanta reputazione, che per se stesso si sarebbe retto, e non sarebbe più dependuto dalla fortuna e forze di altri, ma dalla potenza e virtù sua. Ma Alessandro morì dopo cinque anni ch'elli aveva cominciato a trarre fuora la spada. Lasciollo con lo stato di Romagna solamente asso-

them, which he quickly would have succeeded in doing if Alexander had lived.

And these were his methods in regard to present circumstances. But as for the future, he had to consider, primarily, that a new successor to the Church might not be his friend and might indeed attempt to take away what Alexander had given him. He thought of protecting himself from this in four ways: first, by extinguishing all the blood relatives of those noblemen he had despoiled, in order to prevent the Pope from employing that opportunity; second, by winning to his side all the Roman noblemen, as already mentioned, in order to be able with their aid to keep the Pope in restraint; third, by making the College of Cardinals as much his own college as he possibly could; fourth, by acquiring sufficient strength, before the Pope should die, to allow him to withstand on his own a first encounter. He had achieved three of these four things by the time Alexander died; the fourth he was on his way to achieving, for he killed as many of the despoiled noblemen as he could reach, and very few escaped; he had won over the Roman nobility, and he had a very large section of the college; and as for the acquiring of new power, he had planned to become ruler of Tuscany, and already he was in possession of Perugia and Piombino and had taken Pisa under his protection. And as soon as he no longer needed to be concerned with France (for he no longer had to be, since the French had already been stripped of the kingdom by the Spaniards, so that it was necessary for both of them to buy his friendship), he would have made his assault on Pisa. After this, Lucca and Siena would have quickly surrendered, partly out of spite for the Florentines and partly out of fear, and the Florentines would have had no means of preventing this. If he had succeeded (as he was in the process of succeeding the same year that

lidato, con tutti li altri in aria, intra dua potentissimi eserciti inimici, e malato a morte. Ed era nel duca tanta ferocità e tanta virtù, e sì bene conosceva come gli uomini si hanno a guadagnare o perdere, e tanto erano validi e fondamenti che in sì poco tempo si aveva fatti, che, se lui non avessi avuto quelli eserciti addosso, o lui fussi stato sano, arebbe retto a ogni difficultà. E che e fondamenti sua fussino buoni, si vidde: chè la Romagna lo aspettò più di uno mese; in Roma, ancora che mezzo vivo, stette sicuro; e benchè Baglioni, Vitelli e Orsini venissino in Roma, non ebbono sèguito contro di lui; possè fare, se non chi e' volle, papa, almeno che non fussi chi non voleva. Ma se nella morte di Alessandro lui fussi stato sano, ogni cosa li era facile. E lui mi disse, ne' dì che fu creato Iulio II, che aveva pensato a ciò che potessi nascere morendo el padre, e a tutto aveva trovato remedio, eccetto che non pensò mai, in su la sua morte, di stare ancora lui per morire.

Raccolte io, adunque, tutte le azioni del duca, non saprei reprenderlo; anzi mi pare, come ho fatto, di preporlo imitabile a tutti coloro che per fortuna e con l'armi d'altri sono ascesi allo imperio. Perchè lui, avendo l'animo grande e la sua intenzione alta, non si poteva governare altrimenti; e solo si oppose a' sua disegni la

Alexander died), he would have acquired so much strength and so great a reputation that he would have been able to stand on his own, and no longer would have had to depend on the fortune and strength of others, but rather on his own power and ingenuity. But Alexander died five years after Cesare had started to draw his sword. He left him with only the state of Romagna consolidated, with all the rest up in the air, between two very powerful enemy armies, and deathly ill. And there was in the duke such ferocity and such ingenuity, and so well did he understand how men must be won over or lost, and so sound were the foundations he had laid in so short a time that, if he had not had those armies on his back, or had he been in good health, he would have withstood any difficulty. And that his foundations were good is evident: for Romagna waited more than a month for him; in Rome, though only half alive, he went unharmed; and although the Baglioni, the Vitelli and the Orsini came to Rome, they found none of their followers opposed to him; he could have created the Pope, if not whom he wanted, it would not have been one he did not want. But if at the time of Alexander's death he had been in good health, everything would have been easy for him. And on the day that Julius II was made Pope, he himself said to me that he had thought of what might take place when his father died, and he had found a solution for everything, except he never thought that when his father was at the point of death he too would be about to die.[13]

Having summarized, then, all the accomplishments of the Duke, I would not know how to reprimand him; rather, I feel I have done well in suggesting, as I have, that he be imitated by all those who through fortune and with the arms of others have risen to power. For he, having great courage and lofty intentions, could not have

brevità della vita di Alessandro e la malattia sua. Chi, adunque, iudica necessario nel suo principato nuovo assicurarsi de' nimici, guadagnarsi delli amici, vincere o per forza o per fraude, farsi amare e temere da' populi, sequire e reverire da' soldati, spegnere quelli che ti possano o debbano offendere, innovare con nuovi modi gli ordini antiqui, essere severo e grato, magnanimo e liberale, spegnere la milizia infedele, creare della nuova, mantenere le amicizie de' re e de' principi in modo che ti abbino o a benificare con grazia o offendere con respetto, non può trovare e più freschi esempli che le azioni di costui. Solamente si può accusarlo nella creazione di Iulio pontefice, nella quale lui ebbe mala elezione; perchè, come è detto, non potendo fare uno papa a suo modo, e' poteva tenere che uno non fussi papa; e non doveva mai consentire al papato di quelli cardinali che lui avesi offesi, o che, diventati papi, avessino ad avere paura di lui. Perchè gli uomini offendono o per paura o per odio. Quelli che lui aveva offesi erano, infra li altri, San Piero ad Vincula, Colonna, San Giorgio, Ascanio; tutti li altri, divenuti papi, aveano a temerlo, eccetto Roano e li Spagnuoli: questi per coniunzione e obligo, quello per potenzia, avendo coniunto seco il regno di Francia. Pertanto el duca, innanzi a ogni cosa, doveva creare papa uno spagnolo, e, non potendo, doveva consentire che fussi Roano e non San Piero ad Vincula. E chi crede che ne' personaggi grandi e benefizii nuovi faccino dimenticare le iniurie vecchie, s' inganna. Errò, adunque, el duca in questa elezione, e fu cagione dell' ultima ruina sua.

ruled in any other fashion; and the only thing that opposed his plans was the brevity of Alexander's life and his own sickness. Whoever, then, decides in his new principality to protect himself from his enemies, win friends, conquer either by means of force or fraud, to make himself loved and feared by the people, followed and revered by the soldiers, to do away with those who can and must do him harm, innovate the old traditions with new customs, to be severe and gracious, magnanimous and generous, to do away with unfaithful troops, create new ones, maintain the friendships of kings and princes in such a way that they must assist him with pleasure or offend him with caution, this person will not find more recent examples than the actions of the Duke. Only in making Julius Pope, where he made a bad choice, can he be blamed, because, as I said before, unable to create a Pope of his own, he could have prevented a particular one from becoming Pope; and he should never have consented to the papacy of any cardinal he might have offended, or who, once Pope, might have reason to fear him. For men do harm either out of fear or hate. Those he had offended were, among others, San Pietro ad Vincula, Colonna, San Giorgio, Ascanio; any of the others, if elected Pope, would have had cause to fear him, with the exception of Rohan and the Spaniards: the latter because they were related and obligated to him;[14] the former because of his power, being related and joined to the kingdom of France. And so the Duke above all should have made a Spaniard Pope, and, if unable to do so, he should have consented to Rohan's election and not to that of San Pietro ad Vincula.[15] And whoever believes that with prominent personages new benefits cause old injuries to be forgotten is deceiving himself. The duke, then, made a mistake in this election, and it was the source of his ultimate ruin.

NOTES

1. Darius I, King of the Persians from 521 to 485 B.C., was the most important Persian conqueror after Cyrus.

2. Machiavelli is referring to those Roman emperors who reigned from 161 to 238 A.D. See Chapter XIX.

3. See Chapter I, note 1.

4. Cesare Borgia (1476–1507), the son of Pope Alexander VI, was the protagonist of one of the most exceptional and striking political adventures of the first years of the sixteenth century: after having conquered Rome with the military aid of Louis XII, he sketched a wide plan of conquest of Tuscany and central Italy. At the death of his father (1503), he took refuge with the Spaniards and died in Spain in 1507.

5. He was called Duke Valentino because at one time he ruled the Duchy of Valence in France, bestowed on him by Louis XII after he had resigned his position as cardinal, given him by his father, Alexander VI.

6. Ludovico il Moro.

7. Orsini and Colonna were illustrious Roman families from which came many "condottieri" of the militias. They, among others, were the chief adversaries of the Pope's secular politics.

8. Louis XII was allied to Florence.

9. This conference was called to discuss a way to stop Valentino's rapidly increasing military power; it was attended by such distinguished leaders as Vitelozzo Vitelli, Oliverotto da Fermo, the Orsini, the Bentivogli, and others.

10. Called Sinigallia today (in the province Ancona).

11. Remirro de Orco, the "majordomo" of Cesare Borgia, came with him from France in 1498. He was then named lieutenant general of Romagna in 1501. Imprisoned on December 22, 1502, he was put to death the morning of the 26th.

12. The armies of the Orsini, Colonna and Vitelli.

13. In fact, he died in 1506 at the age of 32.

14. There were eleven Spaniards in the College of Cardinals, all either relatives or close friends of Alexander VI.

15. Known as Giuliano della Rovere (Pope Julius II).

VIII De His Qui Per Scelera ad Principatum Pervenere

Ma perchè di privato si diventa principe ancora in dua modi, il che non si può al tutto o alla fortuna o alla virtù attribuire, non mi pare da lasciarli indrieto, ancora che dell' uno si possa più diffusamente ragionare dove si trattassi delle republiche. Questi sono quando o per qualche via scellerata e nefaria si ascende al principato, o quando uno privato cittadino con il favore delli altri suoi cittadini diventa principe della sua patria. E parlando del primo modo, si mostrerrà con dua esempli, l' uno antiquo, l' altro moderno, sanza entrare altrimenti ne' meriti di questa parte, perchè io iudico che basti, a chi fussi necessitato, imitarli.

Agatocle siciliano, non solo di privata ma di infima e abietta fortuna, divenne re di Siracusa. Costui, nato d' uno figulo, tenne sempre, per li gradi della sua età, vita scellerata; nondimanco, accompagnò le sue scelleratezze con tanta virtù di animo e di corpo, che, voltosi alla milizia, per li gradi di quella pervenne ad essere pretore di Siracusa. Nel quale grado sendo costituito, e avendo deliberato diventare principe e tenere con violenzia e senza obligo d' altri quello che d' accordo gli era suto concesso, e avuto di questo suo disegno intelligenzia con Amilcare cartaginese, il quale con gli eserciti militava in Sicilia, raunò una mattina il populo e il senato di Siracusa, come se egli avessi avuto a deliberare cose pertinenti alla republica e, ad uno cenno ordinato, fece da' sua soldati uccidere tutti e senatori e gli più ricchi del popolo; e quali morti, occupò e tenne il principato di quella città sanza alcuna controversia civile. E benchè da' Cartaginesi fussi dua volte rotto e demum assediato, non solum possè defendere la sua città, ma, lasciato parte delle sua gente alla difesa della obsidione, con le altre assaltò l' Affrica,

VIII On Those Who Have Become Princes Through Iniquity

But[1] since there are still two more ways one can from an ordinary citizen become prince, which cannot be attributed altogether to fortune or ingenuity, I do not think they should be overlooked, even though one of them could be dealt with at more length in a treatise on republics. These are, when one becomes prince by some iniquitous and nefarious way, or when an ordinary citizen becomes prince of his native city with the backing of his fellow citizens. And in speaking of the first way, I shall use two examples, one from antiquity, the other recent, without entering further into the merits of such a way, for I consider them sufficient for anyone obliged to follow them.

Agathocles the Sicilian,[2] not only from an ordinary citizen but from low and abject status, became king of Syracuse. This man, the son of a potter, led an iniquitous life at every stage of his career; however, he coupled his iniquities with such power of mind and body that, when he turned to a military career, he rose through the ranks to become commander of Syracuse. Once elected to such a position, having given thought to becoming prince and to maintaining with violence and without any obligations to others that which had been unanimously conceded to him, and having taken into his confidence Hamilcar the Carthaginian,[3] who was waging war with his armies in Sicily, one morning he called together the people and senators of Syracuse as if he were going to discuss the affairs of state with them; and with a prearranged gesture, he had his soldiers kill all the senators and the richest citizens; once they were dead, he occupied and maintained jurisdiction over that city without any civil strife. And although he was beaten twice by the Carthaginians and finally besieged, not only was he able to defend his

e in breve tempo liberò Siracusa dallo assedio, e condusse e Cartaginesi in estrema necessità: e furono necessitati accordarsi con quello, essere contenti della possessione di Affrica e ad Agatocle lasciare la Sicilia.

Chi considerassi, adunque, le azioni e vita di costui, non vedrà cose, o poche, le quali possa attribuire alla fortuna; con ciò sia cosa, come di sopra è detto, che, non per favore d'alcuno, ma per li gradi della milizia, e quali con mille disagi e periculi si aveva guadagnati, pervenissi al principato, e quello di poi con tanti partiti animosi e periculosi mantenessi. Non si può ancora chiamare virtù ammazzare e sua cittadini, tradire li amici, essere sanza fede, sanza pietà, sanza religione; e quali modi possono fare acquistare imperio, ma non gloria. Perchè se si considerassi la virtù di Agatocle nello entrare e nello uscire de' periculi, e la grandezza dello animo suo nel sopportare e superare le cose avverse, non si vede perchè elli abbi ad essere iudicato inferiore a qualunque eccellentissimo capitano; nondimanco, la sua efferata crudeltà e inumanità, con infinite scelleratezze, non consentono che sia infra li eccellentissimi uomini celebrato. Non si può, adunque, attribuire alla fortuna o alla virtù quello che sanza l'una e l'altra fu da lui consequito.

Ne' tempi nostri, regnante Alessandro VI, Liverotto firmano, sendo più anni innanzi rimaso, piccolo, sanza padre, fu da uno suo zio materno, chiamato Giovanni Fogliani, allevato, e ne' primi tempi della sua gioventù dato a militare sotto Paulo Vitelli, acciò che, ripieno di quella disciplina, pervenissi a qualche eccellente grado di milizia. Morto di poi Paulo, militò sotto Vitellozzo suo fratello; e in brevissimo tempo, per essere ingegnoso, e della persona e dello animo gagliardo, diventò el primo

city, but leaving part of his troops to defend it from besiegers, he invaded Africa with the rest, and in a short time he liberated Syracuse from the siege, and reduced the Carthaginians to dire straits: and they were forced to come to an agreement with him, to be content with possessing Africa and to leave Sicily to Agathocles.[4]

Whoever examines, therefore, the actions and life of this man will find nothing or very little that can be attributed to fortune; for, as was said above, not with the help of others but by advancing in the military ranks, which involved a thousand hardships and dangers, he came to rule the principality which he then managed to maintain by many courageous and dangerous efforts. Yet it cannot be called ingenuity to kill one's fellow citizens, betray friends, be without faith, without pity, without religion; all of these may bring one to power, but not to glory. For if one were to consider the ingenuity of Agathocles in facing and surviving dangers, in his courageous spirit to undergo and overcome adversities, one cannot see why he should be judged inferior to any most outstanding commander; nevertheless, his vicious cruelty and inhumanity, together with his infinite iniquitous deeds, do not allow him to be counted among the most outstanding famous men. One cannot, therefore, attribute to fortune or ingenuity what was achieved by him without either of the two.

In our own day, under the reign of Alexander VI, Oliverotto of Fermo,[5] having been left a fatherless child some years before, was raised by a maternal uncle called Giovanni Fogliani, and in his early youth he was sent to soldier under Paulo Vitelli[6] so that, once skilled in that discipline, he might arrive at an outstanding military position. Then when Paulo died, he trained under Vitellozzo, his brother; and in a very short time, because he was intelligent and courageous in thought as well as in

uomo della sua milizia. Ma parendoli cosa servile lo stare
con altri, pensò, con lo aiuto di alcuni cittadini di Fermo
a' quali era più cara la servitù che la libertà della loro
patria, e con il favore vitellesco, di occupare Fermo; e
scrisse a Giovanni Fogliani come, sendo stato più anni
fuora di casa, voleva venire a vedere lui e la sua città, e
in qualche parte riconoscere el suo patrimonio; e perchè
non si era affaticato per altro che per acquistare onore,
acciò che e suoi cittadini vedessino come non aveva speso
el tempo in vano, voleva venire onorevole e accompagnato da cento cavalli di sua amici e servidori; e pregavalo
fussi contento ordinare che da' Firmani fussi ricevuto
onoratamente; il che non solamente tornava onore a lui,
ma a se proprio, sendo suo allievo. Non mancò, pertanto,
Giovanni di alcuno offizio debito verso el nipote; e, fat-
tolo ricevere da' Firmani onoratamente, si alloggiò nelle
case sua; dove, passato alcuno giorno, e atteso ad ordinare
secretamente quello che alla sua futura scelleratezza era
necessario, fece uno convito solennissimo, dove invitò
Giovanni Fogliani e tutti e primi uomini di Fermo. E
consumate che furno le vivande e tutti gli altri intratteni-
menti che in simili conviti si usano, Liverotto, ad arte,
mosse certi ragionamenti gravi, parlando della grandezza
di papa Alessandro e di Cesare suo figliuolo, e delle imprese loro. A' quali ragionamenti respondendo Giovanni
e gli altri, lui a un tratto si rizzò, dicendo quelle essere
cose da parlarne in loco più secreto; e ritirossi in una
camera, dove Giovanni e tutti gli altri cittadini li andorno
drieto. Nè prima furono posti a sedere, che de' luoghi
secreti di quella uscirono soldati, che ammazzorno Giovanni e tutti gli altri. Dopo il quale omicidio, montò
Liverotto a cavallo, e corse la terra, e assediò nel palazzo
el supremo magistrato; tanto che, per paura, furono costretti obedirlo, e fermare uno governo del quale si fece

action, he became the leader of his troops. But considering it a servile thing to work for others, he made up his mind, with the help of some citizens of Fermo who cherished slavery more than the liberty of their native land, and with the backing of Vitellozzo's followers, to take possession of Fermo; and he wrote to Giovanni Fogliano how, having been away from home for so many years, he wished to return to see him and his city and to appraise his inheritance; and since he had sought only to win honor, so that his fellow citizens would see that he had not wasted his time, he wished to arrive in honorable fashion accompanied by one hundred of his friends and followers on horseback; and he requested that the people of Fermo prepare an honorable reception, one that would do honor not only to Giovanni but also to himself, his charge. Giovanni, accordingly, in no way failed in the proper reception of his nephew, and he saw to it that the people of Fermo received him in honorable fashion, and lodged him in his own house; where, after a few days Oliverotto, having secretly made the preparations necessary to his forthcoming iniquity, gave a very elegant banquet to which he invited Giovanni Fogliani and all the leading men of Fermo. And when the meal and the entertainment customary at such banquets was over, Oliverotto, in a clever way, began to discuss certain delicate matters, speaking of the greatness of Pope Alexander and his son Cesare and their enterprises. While Giovanni and the others were taking part in the discussion, he suddenly rose to his feet saying that these were matters to be spoken of in a more secluded place; and he withdrew to a room followed by Giovanni and all the other citizens. No sooner were they seated than from secret places in that room soldiers came out and murdered Giovanni and all the others. After this homicide, Oliverotto mounted his

principe. E morti tutti quelli che, per essere mal contenti, lo potevono offendere, si corroborò con nuovi ordini civili e militari; in modo che, in spazio d'uno anno che tenne el principato, non solamente lui era sicuro nella città di Fermo, ma era diventato pauroso a tutti e sua vicini. E sarebbe suta la sua espugnazione difficile come quella di Agatocle, se non si fussi lasciato ingannare da Cesare Borgia, quando a Sinigaglia, come di sopra si disse, prese li Orsini e Vitelli; dove, preso ancora lui, in uno anno dopo el commisso parricidio, fu, insieme con Vitellozzo, il quale aveva avuto maestro delle virtù e scelleratezze sua, strangolato.

Potrebbe alcuno dubitare donde nascessi che Agatocle e alcuno simile, dopo infiniti tradimenti e crudeltà, possè vivere lungamente sicuro nella sua patria e defendersi dalli inimici esterni, e da' sua cittadini non gli fu mai cospirato contro; con ciò sia che molti altri, mediante la crudeltà, non abbino, etiam ne' tempi pacifici, possuto mantenere lo stato, non che ne' tempi dubbiosi di guerra. Credo che questo avvenga dalle crudeltà male usate o bene usate. Bene usate si possono chiamare quelle (se del male è licito dire bene) che si fanno a un tratto, per la necessità dello assicurarsi, e di poi non vi si insiste drento, ma si convertiscono in più utilità de' sudditi che si può; male usate sono quelle le quali, ancora che nel principio sieno poche, più tosto con el tempo crescono che le si spenghino. Coloro che osservano el primo modo, possono con Dio e con li uomini avere allo stato loro qualche remedio, come ebbe Agatocle; quelli altri è impossibile si mantenghino.

horse, paraded through the town, and besieged the palace of the government; so that through fear they were forced to obey him and form a government of which he became the master. And once all those were dead who, because they were unhappy, could hurt him, he strengthened himself with new civil and military laws; so that, in the space of the year that he held his princedom, not only was he secure in the city of Fermo but he had become feared by all his neighboring states. And his expulsion would have been as difficult as that of Agathocles had he not allowed himself to be deceived by Cesare Borgia when at Sinigaglia, as was mentioned above, he captured the Orsini and Vitelli; where he too was captured, a year after he committed the parricide, and, together with Vitellezzo, who had been his teacher in strategy and crime, was strangled.

One might question how Agathocles and others like him, after so many treacheries and cruelties, could live for a long time secure in their country and defend themselves from outside enemies without being conspired against by their own citizens; while many others, because of their cruelty, were unable, even in time of peace, to hold their power, not to mention the unstable times of war. I believe this depends on cruelty being badly or well used. Those cruelties can be considered well used (if it is permissible to say good about the bad) that are performed all at once, in order to assure one's position, and are not continued, but rather turned to the greatest advantage as possible for the subjects. Badly used are those cruelties that, although at first they are few, increase with time rather than disappear. Those who observe the first way can remedy their position with God and man as Agathocles did; the others will find it impossible to survive.

Onde è da notare che, nel pigliare uno stato, debbe l'occupatore di esso discorrere tutte quelle offese che gli è necessario fare, e tutte farle a uno tratto, per non le avere a rinnovare ogni dì, e potere, non le innovando, assicurare gli uomini e guadagnarseli con benificarli. Chi fa altrimenti, o per timidità o per mal consiglio, è sempre necessitato tenere el coltello in mano; nè mai può fondarsi sopra e sua sudditi, non si potendo quelli, per le fresche e continue iniurie, assicurare di lui. Perchè le iniurie si debbano fare tutte insieme, acciò che, assaporandosi meno, offendino meno; e benefizii si debbano fare a poco a poco, acciò si assaporino meglio. E debbe, sopra tutto, uno principe vivere con li suoi sudditi in modo che veruno accidente o di male o di bene lo abbi a fare variare; perchè, venendo, per li tempi avversi, le necessità, tu non se' a tempo al male; e il bene che tu fai non ti giova, perchè è iudicato forzato, e non te n' è saputo grado alcuno.

NOTES

1. Connects with Chapter VI, where Machiavelli says, ". . . since this event, of transition from ordinary citizen to prince, presupposes either ingenuity or fortune . . ."

2. Agathocles was the tyrant of Syracuse from 316–289 B.C. who fought against the Carthaginians in Africa.

3. Hamilcar the Carthaginian (Hamilcar Barca) had fought as head of the Carthaginians against Agathocles in defense of Syracuse.

Whereby it should be noted that in capturing a state the conqueror should consider all the injuries he must inflict, and inflict all of them at once, so as not to have to repeat them daily, and in not repeating them to be able to give men a feeling of security and win them over with the benefits he offers. Whoever does otherwise, whether through timidity or bad advice, will always have to keep knife in hand; nor will he ever be able to count on his subjects, who, because of their fresh and continuous injuries, cannot feel secure with him. Injuries, then, should be inflicted all at once, for the less they are tasted the less they offend; benefits should be distributed little by little so they may be better tasted. And a prince should, above all, live with his subjects in such a way that no unforeseen event whether good or bad make him change his course; for should the need to change arise because of adverse conditions, you are not in time to resort to the bad, and the good you do will gain you nothing, for it will be considered a necessary measure, and earn you no gratitude.

4. Not all of Sicily; only the Greek portion.

5. Oliverotto, whom Cesare Borgia had strangled in Sinigallia in 1502, a year after he had become Lord of Fermo, attained the position by the iniquitous means here described.

6. Paulo Vitelli was the brother of the same Vitellozzo whom Cesare Borgia also had strangled at Sinigallia. He was one of the most famous mercenary captains of his time, and held charge of the Florentine armies in the war against Pisa. He was decapitated on suspicion of treason on October 1, 1499.

Ma venendo all'altra parte, quando uno privato cittadino, non per scelleratezza o altra intollerabile violenzia,
ma con il favore delli altri sua cittadini diventa principe
della sua patria (il quale si può chiamare principato civile;
nè a pervenirvi è necessario o tutta virtù o tutta fortuna,
ma più presto una astuzia fortunata) dico che si ascende
a questo principato o con il favore del populo o con
quello de' grandi. Perchè in ogni città si truovono questi
dua umori diversi; e nasce da questo, che il populo desidera non essere comandato nè oppresso da' grandi, e li
grandi desiderano comandare e opprimere el populo; e
da questi dua appetiti diversi nasce nelle città uno de' tre
effetti: o principato o libertà o licenzia.

El principato è causato o dal populo o da' grandi,
secondo che l'una o l'altra di queste parte ne ha la occasione. Perchè, vedendo e grandi non potere resistere al
populo, cominciano a voltare la reputazione a uno di loro;
e fannolo principe per potere, sotto la sua ombra, sfogare
il loro appetito. El populo ancora, vedendo non potere
resistere a' grandi, volta la reputazione a uno, e lo fa
principe per essere, con la autorità sua, difeso. Colui che
viene al principato con lo aiuto de' grandi, si mantiene
con più difficultà che quello che diventa con lo aiuto del
populo; perchè si truova principe con di molti intorno
che gli paiano essere sua equali, e per questo non gli può
nè comandare nè maneggiare a suo modo. Ma colui che
arriva al principato con il favore popolare, vi si truova
solo, e ha intorno o nessuno o pochissimi che non sieno
parati a obedire. Oltre a questo, non si può con onestà
satisfare a' grandi e sanza iniuria d'altri, ma sì bene al
populo; perchè quello del populo è più onesto fine che

IX   On the Civil Principality

But now coming to the other situation, when a private citizen, not through iniquity or any other intolerable means of violence, but with the help of his fellow citizens, becomes prince of his country (and this may be called a civil principality, the attainment of which depends neither entirely on ingenuity or fortune but rather on a combination of astuteness and luck), let me say that one attains this principality either with the help of the common people or the nobles. For these two different tendencies are found in every city and arise from the fact that the common people do not wish to be governed nor oppressed by the nobles, and the nobles wish to govern and oppress the common people; and from these two diverse desires there arise in cities one of three effects: a principality or freedom or anarchy.

A principality is created either by the common people or the nobles, depending on which of these two factions has the opportunity. For when the nobles see that they cannot hold out against the common people, they begin to build up the prestige of one of their own and make him prince in order to be able, under his protection, to satisfy their desires. The common people, in the same way, seeing they cannot hold out against the nobles, build up the prestige of one of their own and make him prince in order to have the defense of his authority. He who becomes prince with the help of the nobles sustains his position with more difficulty than he who becomes prince with the help of the common people; for he will find himself a prince surrounded by many who believe they are his equals, and for this reason he can neither govern nor handle them as he would like to. But he who is made prince with the support of the common people will find himself all alone, surrounded by no one or very few who

quello de' grandi, volendo questi opprimere e quello non essere oppresso. Praeterea, del populo inimico uno principe non si può mai assicurare, per essere troppi; de' grandi si può assicurare, per essere pochi. El peggio che possa espettare uno principe dal populo inimico, è lo essere abbandonato da lui; ma da' grandi, inimici, non solo debbe temere di essere abbandonato, ma etiam che loro li venghino contro; perchè, sendo in quelli più vedere e più astuzia, avanzono sempre tempo per salvarsi, e cercano gradi con quello che sperano che vinca. È necessitato ancora el principe vivere sempre con quello medesimo populo; ma può ben fare sanza quelli medesimi grandi, potendo farne e disfarne ogni dì, e torre e dare, a sua posta, reputazione loro.

E per chiarire meglio questa parte, dico come e grandi si debbano considerare in dua modi principalmente: o si governano in modo, col procedere loro, che si obligano in tutto alla tua fortuna, o no. Quelli che si obligano, e non sieno rapaci, si debbano onorare e amare; quelli che non si obligano, si hanno ad esaminare in dua modi: o fanno questo per pusillanimità e defetto naturale di animo; allora tu ti debbi servire di quelli massime che sono di buono consiglio, perchè nelle prosperità te ne onori, e non hai nelle avversità da temerne. Ma quando e' non si obligano ad arte e per cagione ambiziosa, è segno come pensano più a sè che a te; e da quelli si debbe el principe guardare, e temerli come se fussino scoperti inimici, perchè sempre, nelle avversità, aiuteranno ruinarlo.

are not ready to obey him. Besides this, it is impossible for the nobles to be satisfied in an honest way without doing harm to others, but the common people certainly can be, for the goal of the common people is more honest than that of the nobles, the latter wishing to oppress and the former wishing not to be oppressed. In addition, a prince can never be safe when the common people are his enemy, for there are so many of them; he can be safe with the nobles, for there are so few of them. The worst that a prince can expect from a hostile people is to be abandoned by them; but with the nobles as his enemies, not only must he fear their abandoning him but also their turning against him, for possessing more foresight and more shrewdness, they are always in time to save themselves and seek the favors of the side they hope will win. Furthermore, a prince must always live with the same common people; but he certainly can do without the same nobles, for he can create them and destroy them from one day to the next, as well as take away and give them their prestige as he pleases.

To clarify this part more fully, let me say that the nobles should be considered mainly in two ways: either they conduct themselves in such a way that they wholly ally themselves to your fortunes or they do not. Those who ally themselves and are not greedy should be honored and loved; those who do not ally themselves can be analyzed in two ways. They act this way out of cowardice and a natural lack of courage, in which case you should make use of them, especially of those who are wise counselors, for in times of prosperity they will bring you honor and in adverse times you have nothing to fear from them; however, when they do not ally themselves to you for a definite reason and for ambitious purposes, it is a sign that they are thinking more about themselves than about you; and the prince should watch out for such men, and

Debbe, pertanto, uno che diventi principe mediante il favore del populo, mantenerselo amico; il che gli fia facile, non dimandando lui se non di non essere oppresso. Ma uno che, contro al populo, diventi principe con il favore de' grandi, debbe, innanzi a ogni altra cosa, cercare di guadagnarsi el populo; il che gli fia facile, quando pigli la protezione sua. E perchè li uomini, quando hanno bene da chi credevano avere male, si obligano più al beneficatore loro, diventa el populo subito più suo benivolo che se si fussi condotto al principato con li favori suoi. E puòsselo el principe guadagnare in molti modi, li quali, perchè variano secondo el subietto, non se ne può dare certa regola; e però si lasceranno indrieto. Concluderò solo che a uno principe è necessario avere el populo amico; altrimenti non ha, nelle avversità, remedio.

Nabide, principe delli Spartani, sostenne la obsidione di tutta Grecia e di uno esercito romano vittoriosissimo, e difese contro a quelli la patria sua e il suo stato; e gli bastò solo, sopravvenente el periculo, assicurarsi di pochi: che se egli avessi avuto el populo inimico, questo non li bastava. E non sia alcuno che repugni a questa mia opinione con quello proverbio trito, che chi fonda in sul populo fonda in sul fango; perchè quello è vero quando uno cittadino privato vi fa su fondamento, e dassi a intendere che il populo lo liberi quando e' fussi oppresso da' nimici o da' magistrati (in questo caso si potrebbe trovare spesso ingannato, come a Roma e Gracchi e a Firenze messer Giorgio Scali); ma sendo uno principe

he should fear them as if they were open enemies, because in adverse times without fail they will help bring about his downfall.

One who becomes prince through the support of the common people, however, should maintain their friendship, which should be easy for him, since the only thing they ask of him is that they not be oppressed. But one who, contrary to the wishes of the common people, becomes prince with the help of the nobles should, above all else, try to win over the common people, which should be easy for him once he takes them into his protection. And since all men, when they are well treated by someone they expected would treat them badly, are more bound to their benefactor, the common people will quickly become more inclined to him than if he became prince with their help. And a prince can win over the common people in many ways, but since these ways vary according to circumstances, no fixed rules can be established, and therefore I shall not discuss them. I shall conclude by saying only that a prince must keep on friendly terms with the common people; otherwise, in adverse times, he will find no assistance.

Nabis,[1] prince of the Spartans, resisted the attacks of all of Greece as well as one of Rome's most victorious armies, and he defended his country and his reign against them; and when danger was imminent he had only to protect himself from very few of his subjects: but if he had had the common people against him, this would not have been enough. And let no one contradict my convictions with that trite proverb, "Who builds on the people builds on the mud"; because that holds true when a private citizen lays his foundations there and lets himself believe that the people will liberate him should he be oppressed by the enemy or by the magistrates (in this case, a man could often find himself deceived, like the

che vi fondi su, che possi comandare, e sia uomo di core
nè si sbigottisca nelle avversità, e non manchi delle altre
preparazioni, e tenga con lo animo e ordini suoi animato
lo universale, mai si troverrà ingannato da lui, e li parrà
avere fatti li sua fondamenti buoni.

Sogliono questi principati periclitare quando sono per
salire dallo ordine civile allo assoluto. Perchè questi principi, o comandano per loro medesimi, o per mezzo de'
magistrati; nell'ultimo caso, è più debole e più periculoso
lo stare loro, perchè gli stanno al tutto con la volontà di
quelli cittadini che sono preposti a' magistrati; li quali,
massime ne' tempi avversi, li possono torre con facilità
grande lo stato, o con farli contro o con non lo obedire.
E il principe non è a tempo, ne' periculi, a pigliare la
autorità assoluta, perchè gli cittadini e sudditi, che sogliono avere e comandamenti da' magistrati, non sono,
in quelli frangenti, per obedire a' sua; e arà sempre, ne'
tempi dubbii, penuria di chi lui si possi fidare. Perchè
simile principe non può fondarsi sopra quello che vede
ne' tempi quieti, quando e cittadini hanno bisogno dello
stato; perchè allora ognuno corre, ognuno promette, e
ciascuno vuole morire per lui, quando la morte è discosto;
ma ne' tempi avversi, quando lo stato ha bisogno de'
cittadini, allora se ne truova pochi. E tanto più è questa
esperienzia periculosa, quanto la non si può fare se non
una volta. E però uno principe savio debba pensare uno
modo per il quale e sua cittadini, sempre e in ogni qualità
di tempo, abbino bisogno dello stato e di lui; e sempre
poi li saranno fedeli.

Gracchi[2] in Rome and Messer Giorgio Scali[3] in Florence); but when the prince who lays his foundations on the people is one who is able to command, and is a man of courage who is not bewildered by adversity, and does not lack other necessities, and who by his courage and the regulations he has established is able to keep his community stimulated, he will never find himself deceived by the people; and he shall see that he has laid good foundations.

Principalities of this kind are usually in danger when they are at the point of changing from a civil to an absolute form of government. For these princes rule either on their own or by means of magistrates; in the latter case the prince's position is weaker and more dangerous for he remains entirely under the will of those citizens who are appointed magistrates: they can, especially in adverse times, very easily seize his power either by openly opposing him or by not obeying him. And in such danger the prince is no longer in time to take absolute control, because the citizens and subjects who are used to taking orders from the magistrates will not, at such crises, obey his; and in uncertain times he will always find a scarcity of people he can trust. Therefore, such a prince cannot count on what he observes during tranquil times, when the citizens need his state, for then everyone comes running, everyone makes promises, and each one is willing to give up his life for the prince, the possibility of death being so remote; but in adverse times, when the state needs its citizens, then so few are to be found. And this experiment is all the more dangerous in that it cannot be performed more than once. And so a wise prince must think of a way by which his citizens, at all times and in every kind of situation, will feel the need for the state and for himself; and then they will be forever faithful to him.

NOTES

1. Nabis, tyrant of Sparta from 205–192 B.C., imposed himself as king and succeeded in maintaining his position even after the defeat inflicted by the Romans in 195.

2. The Gracchi, Tiberius and Gaius Sempronius, brothers and tribunes of the Roman people, favored a political democracy. Tiberius was slain in an uprising in 133 B.C.; Gaius had himself killed by one of his slaves in 121 B.C. so as not to die at the hands of his enemies.

3. Giorgio Scali, a rich citizen of Florence, after the tumult of the Ciompi (1378) became, along with Tommaso Strozzi, head of the people. However, the insolence of both and the hatred of their enemies drove Scali to death in 1382 and Strozzi to flight.

X Quomodo Omnium Principatuum Vires Perpendi Debeant

Conviene avere, nello esaminare le qualità di questi principati, un'altra considerazione: cioè, se uno principe ha tanto stato che possa, bisognando, per se medesimo reggersi; o vero se ha sempre necessità della defensione di altri. E per chiarire meglio questa parte, dico come io iudico coloro potersi reggere per se medesimi, che possono, o per abundanzia di uomini o di danari, mettere insieme uno esercito iusto e fare una giornata con qualunque li viene ad assaltare; e così iudico coloro avere sempre necessità di altri, che non possono comparire contro al nimico in campagna, ma sono necessitati rifuggirsi drento alle mura e guardare quelle. Nel primo caso, si è discorso e per lo avvenire direno quello ne occorre; nel secondo caso non si può dire altro, salvo che confortare tali principi a fortificare e munire la terra propria, e del paese non tenere alcuno conto. E qualunque arà bene fortificata la sua terra, e circa li altri governi con li sudditi si fia maneggiato come di sopra è detto e di sotto si dirà, sarà sempre con gran rispetto assaltato; perchè gli uomini sono sempre nimici delle imprese dove si vegga difficultà, nè si può vedere facilità assaltando uno che abbi la sua terra gagliarda e non sia odiato dal populo.

Le città di Alamagna sono liberissime, hanno poco contado, e obediscano allo imperadore quando le vogliono, e non temono nè quello nè altro potente che le abbino intorno; perchè le sono in modo fortificate, che ciascuno pensa la espugnazione di esse dovere essere tediosa e difficile. Perchè tutte hanno fossi e mura convenienti; hanno artiglieria a sufficienzia; tengono sempre nelle canove pubbliche da bere e da mangiare e da ardere per uno anno; e oltre a questo, per potere tenere la plebe pasciuta

X How the Strength of All Principalities Should Be Determined

In examining the characteristics of these principalities, another consideration must be taken up; that is, whether a prince has enough power to enable him, should the necessity arise, to stand on his own, or whether he is constantly in need of the protection of others. And better to clarify this section let me say that I consider self-sufficient those who, whether through abundance of men or money, are able to put together an adequate army and fight a good battle against whoever should attack them; and I consider those who always need the protection of others to be those who cannot meet their enemy on the field of battle but must take refuge within the walls and defend them. The first case has already been discussed and further on I shall say whatever else seems appropriate. Nothing can be said concerning the second except to encourage such princes to fortify and provide for their city and pay no attention to the surrounding countryside. And whoever has properly fortified his city and conducted his relationships with his subjects in the manner I mentioned above, and will speak of below, will be attacked only after much deliberation; for men are always wary of an enterprise that shows its dangers, and it cannot appear easy to attack someone whose city is a fortress and who is not hated by the people.

The cities of Germany are entirely free, possess little land, and obey the emperor when they choose, and they fear neither him nor any other neighboring power; for they are fortified in such a way that everyone thinks that to destroy them would be prolonged and difficult. For they all have adequate moats and walls; they have the necessary artillery; they always keep the public storehouses stocked with food and drink and fuel to last a year; and besides this, to provide for the lower classes without bur-

e sanza perdita del pubblico, hanno sempre in comune, per uno anno, da potere dare loro da lavorare in quelli esercizii che sieno il nervo e la vita di quella città, e delle industrie de' quali la plebe pasca. Tengono ancora li esercizii militari in reputazione, e sopra questo hanno molti ordini a mantenerli.

Uno principe, adunque, che abbi una città forte e non si facci odiare, non può essere assaltato; e se pure fussi chi lo assaltassi, se ne partirebbe con vergogna; perchè le cose del mondo sono sì varie, che gli è quasi impossibile che uno potessi con li eserciti stare uno anno ozioso a campeggiarlo. E chi replicassi: se il populo arà le sue possessioni fuora, e veggale ardere, non ci arà pazienza; e il lungo assedio e la carità propria li farà sdimenticare el principe; respondo che uno principe potente e animoso supererà sempre tutte quelle difficultà, dando a' sudditi ora speranza che il male non fia lungo, ora timore della crudeltà del nimico, ora assicurandosi con destrezza di quelli che gli paressino troppo arditi. Oltre a questo, el nimico, ragionevolmente debba ardere e ruinare el paese in su la sua giunta, e ne' tempi quando li animi degli uomini sono ancora caldi e volonterosi alla difesa; e però tanto meno el principe debbe dubitare, perchè dopo qualche giorno, che li animi sono raffreddi, sono di già fatti e danni, sono ricevuti e mali, e non vi è più remedio; e allora tanto più si vengono a unire con il loro principe, parendo che lui abbi, con loro, obligo, sendo loro sute arse le case, ruinate le possessioni, per la difesa sua. E la natura delli uomini è, così obligarsi per li benefizii che si fanno come per quelli che si ricevano. Onde, se si considerrà bene tutto, non fia difficile a uno principe prudente tenere, prima e poi, fermi gli animi de' sua cittadini nella obsidione, quando non li manchi da vivere nè da difendersi.

dening public finances, they always have a year's supply
of raw materials to provide these people with work in
those crafts that are the sinews and life of that city, and
by which the common people make their living. Moreover, military exercises are still highly regarded, and they
have many regulations to maintain them.

A prince, then, who has a strong city and does not
make himself hated cannot be attacked; and even if he
should be attacked, the besieger would have to retreat
in shame, because human events are so changeable that
it is almost impossible that one maintain a siege for a
year with his troops idle. And to whoever might respond:
if the people have their possessions outside the walls and
see them burned they will lose patience, and the long
siege and self-interest will make them forget about the
prince, let me answer that a powerful and courageous
prince will always manage to overcome all these difficulties by inspiring his subjects, now with the hope that
these bad times will not last long, now by instilling in
them the fear of the enemy's cruelty, now by taking
shrewd steps to protect himself from those who seem too
outspoken. Besides this, the enemy will normally burn
and ravage the surrounding countryside as soon as he
arrives, at a time when men's minds are still ardent and
enthusiastic for the defense; and so the prince has even
less to fear, because, after several days, when men's minds
have begun to cool, the damage has already been done,
the evil suffered, and there is no way of undoing it; and
now the people more than ever will rally to unite with
their prince, who would seem bound in obligation to
them since their houses were burned and their possessions ravaged in his defense. And human nature is such
that men find themselves bound in obligation as much
through the benefits they bestow as through those they

receive. Therefore, taking all this into consideration, it should not be difficult for a wise prince to keep up the spirits of his citizens from the beginning to the end of a siege, just so long as the necessary food and defenses are not lacking.

Restaci solamente, al presente, a ragionare de' principati ecclesiastici; circa quali tutte le difficultà sono avanti che si possegghino; perchè si acquistano o per virtù o per fortuna, e sanza l'una e l'altra si mantengano; perchè sono sustentati dalli ordini antiquati nella religione, quali sono suti tanto potenti e di qualità che tengono e loro principi in stato, in qualunque modo si procedino e vivino. Costoro soli hanno stati, e non gli defendano; suddili, e non gli governano; e gli stati, per essere indifesi, non sono loro tolti; e li suddili, per non essere governati, non se ne curano, nè pensano nè possono alienarsi da loro. Solo, adunque, questi principati sono sicuri e felici. Ma sendo quelli retti da cagione superiori, alle quali mente umana non aggiugne, lascerò il parlarne; perchè, sendo esaltati e mantenuti da Dio, sarebbe offizio di uomo prosuntuoso e temerario discorrerne. Nondimanco, se alcuno mi ricercassi donde viene che la Chiesa, nel temporale, sia venuta a tanta grandezza, con ciò sia che da Alessandro indrieto e potentati italiani, e non solum quelli che si chiamavono e potentati, ma ogni barone e signore, benchè minimo, quanto al temporale, la estimava poco, e ora uno re di Francia ne trema, e lo ha possuto cavare di Italia e ruinare e Viniziani; la qual cosa, ancora che sia nota, non mi pare superfluo ridurla in buona parte alla memoria.

Avanti che Carlo re di Francia passassi in Italia, era questa provincia sotto lo imperio del papa, Viniziani, re di Napoli, duca di Milano e Fiorentini. Questi potentati avevano ad avere due cure principali: l'una, che uno forestiero non entrassi in Italia con le arme; l'altra, che veruno di loro occupassi più stato. Quelli a chi si aveva

Now there only remain to be discussed the ecclesiastical principalities, concerning which all the difficulties occur before they are possessed; for they are acquired either through ingenuity or fortune, and maintained without either; for they are maintained through the ancient ordinances of religion, which are so powerful and of such quality that they keep their princes in power no matter how they carry on and conduct their lives. These are the only princes that possess states and do not defend them, that possess subjects and do not govern them; and the states, by remaining undefended, are not taken from them; and the subjects, by not being governed, do not mind it, and they do not hope nor are they able to break their ties with them. These princes, then, are the only safe and happy ones. But since they are supported by superior causes that the human mind is unable to rise to, I shall not speak about them; for, exhalted and maintained as they are by God, to discuss them would be the task of a presumptuous and foolhardy man. However, someone might ask me how the Church has come into temporal power of such magnitude when up to the time of Alexander[1] the Italian rulers—not only those who were the recognized rulers but every baron and lord, even the most insignificant—regarded its temporal power as negligible, and now a king of France trembles before it and it has been able to throw him out of Italy[2] and to crush the Venetians;[3] though all this may already be known, I do not consider it superfluous to recall a good deal of it to mind.

Before Charles, king of France, came into Italy,[4] this country was under the control of the Pope, the Venetians, the king of Naples, the duke of Milan, and the Florentines. These rulers had to keep two major concerns in view: one, that a foreigner not enter Italy with his troops; the other, that no one among themselves extend

più cura, erano Papa e Viniziani. E a tenere indrieto e Viniziani, bisognava la unione di tutti gli altri, come fu nella difesa di Ferrara; e a tenere basso el Papa, si servivano de' baroni di Roma; e quali, sendo divisi in due fazioni, Orsini e Colonnesi, sempre vi era cagione di scandolo fra loro; e stando con le arme in mano in su li occhi al pontefice, tenevano el pontificato debole e infermo. E benchè surgessi qualche volta uno papa animoso, come fu Sisto, tamen la fortuna o il sapere non lo possè mai disobligare da queste incommodità. E la brevità della vita loro ne era cagione; perchè in dieci anni che, ragguagliato, viveva uno papa, a fatica che potessi sbassare una delle fazioni; e se, verbigrazia, l'uno aveva quasi spenti e Colonnesi, surgeva uno altro inimico alli Orsini, che li faceva resurgere, e gli Orsini non era a tempo a spegnere.

Questo faceva che le forze temporali del papa erano poco stimate in Italia. Surse di poi Alessandro VI, il quale, di tutti e pontefici che sono stati mai, mostrò quanto uno papa, e con il danaio e con le forze, si posseva prevalere; e fece, con lo instrumento del duca Valentino e con la occasione della passata de' Franzesi, tutte quelle cose che io discorro di sopra nelle azioni del duca. E benchè lo intento suo non fussi fare grande la Chiesa, ma il duca, nondimeno ciò che fece tornò a grandezza della Chiesa; la quale, dopo la sua morte, spento el duca, fu erede delle sua fatiche. Venne di poi papa Iulio; e trovò la Chiesa grande, avendo tutta la Romagna, e sendo spenti e baroni di Roma e, per le battiture di Alessandro, annullate quelle fazioni; e trovò ancora la via aperta al modo dello accumulare danari, non mai più usitato da Alessandro indrieto. Le quali cose Iulio non solum seguitò, ma accrebbe; e pensò a guadagnarsi Bologna, e spegnere

his domain. Those to be worried about the most were the Pope and the Venetians. And to hold back the Venetians, the unification of all the others was necessary, as was the case in the defense of Ferrara;[5] and to hold down the Pope, they used the barons of Rome who, divided into two factions, the Orsini and the Colonna, always had a reason for quarreling between themselves, and standing with arms in hand right under the eyes of the Pope, kept the papacy weak and insecure. And even though from time to time there arose a courageous pope, like Sixtus,[6] neither fortune nor wisdom could free him from these difficulties. And the short lives of the popes was the cause of it; for, in ten years, the average life span of a pope, he might with difficulty suppress one of the factions; and if, for instance, one pope had almost done away with the Colonna, a new pope who was hostile to the Orsini would take his place allowing the Colonna to rise again, yet without enough time to do away with the Orsini.

This caused the temporal powers of the pope to be little respected in Italy. Then there rose to power Alexander VI, who, more than any other pope, demonstrated how much a pope, with money and arms, could prevail; and he achieved, with Duke Valentino as his means and the coming of the French as his occasion, all those things I mentioned previously when discussing the actions of the duke.[7] And even though his intention was not to aggrandize the Church but rather the duke, nevertheless what he did resulted in the aggrandizement of the Church which, after his death and once the duke was done away with, became the heir of his labors. Then came Pope Julius;[8] and he found the Church powerful, possessing all of Romagna, with the barons of Rome beaten, and those factions annihilated under the blows struck by Alexander; and, still more, he found the way open for accumulating wealth, a way never before taken by Alexander or his

e Viniziani, e a cacciare e Franzesi di Italia; e tutte queste
imprese li riuscirono, e con tanta più sua laude, quanto
fece ogni cosa per accrescere la Chiesa e non alcuno
privato. Mantenne ancora le parti Orsine e Colonnese in
quelli termini che le trovò; e benchè tra loro fussi qualche
capo da fare alterazione, tamen dua cose gli ha tenuti
fermi: l' una, la grandezza della Chiesa, che gli sbigottisce;
l' altra, el non avere loro cardinali, e quali sono origine
de' tumulti infra loro. Nè mai staranno quiete queste
parti, qualunque volta abbino cardinali; perchè questi
nutriscono, in Roma e fuora, le parti, e quelli baroni sono
forzati a defenderle; e così dalla ambizione de' prelati
nascono le discordie e tumulti infra e baroni. Ha trovato,
adunque, la Santità di papa Leone questo pontificato
potentissimo; el quale si spera, se quelli lo feciono grande
con le armi, questo, con la bontà e infinite altre sue virtù,
lo farà grandissimo e venerando.

NOTES

1. Alexander vi, pope from 1492–1503.
2. The Papacy, by joining with Spain and Venice in the
Lega Santa, helped to drive the French out of Italy in 1513.
3. By participating in the League of Cambrai (1508) which
was directed against the Venetians.
4. In 1494.
5. The reference is the coalition of the Este of Ferrara,
Naples, Florence, Milan, Mantua, and Pope Sixtus.
6. Sixtus, pope from 1471–1484, was born Francesco della
Rovere of humble origin and was elected Pope Sixtus iv at the
death of Paul ii. The brave and unprejudiced initiator of the
political secular rebirth of the Church, he was greatly admired
by Machiavelli. Giuliano della Rovere, the future Pope Julius ii,
was his nephew.

predecessors. These measures Julius not only continued to practice but he added to them: and he thought of winning over Bologna[9] and crushing the Venetians and chasing the French out of Italy; and in all these enterprises he was successful; and he is all the more praiseworthy, as he did everything for the greater advancement of the Church and not for any special individual. Moreover, he managed to keep the Orsini and Colonna factions in the same condition he found them; and although several leaders among them wanted to make changes, there were two things that kept them quiet: one, the power of the Church, which overwhelmed them; the other, not having their own cardinals,[10] who were the cause of the conflict between them. These factions will never be at rest as long as they have cardinals, for they nourish factions, both in Rome and outside it, and those barons are forced to defend them: and so, from the ambitions of the prelates are born the discords and conflicts between the barons. Now His Holiness Pope Leo[11] has found the papacy extremely powerful; and we hope that, just as those before him made it great by means of arms, he, through his bounty and his infinite virtues, will make it very great and worthy of reverence.

7. See Chapter vii.

8. Julius ii, pope from 1503–1513, was an ambitious figure of brave and frenzied politics and advocate of the League of Cambrai against Venice (1508) and of the Lega Santa against Louis xii (1511). He succeeded Pius iii who reigned briefly (September 22 through October 18, 1503) after Alexander vi.

9. This enterprise proved to be successful in 1506.

10. That is to say, not any of their own family in the College of Cardinals.

11. Leo x (Giovanni de' Medici, son of Lorenzo de' Medici) was elected pope on February 21, 1513 and was in power until 1521. He continued to increase the prestige of the Church, as both statesman and patron of the arts.

Avendo discorso particularmente tutte le qualità di quelli principati de' quali nel principio proposi di ragionare, e considerato in qualche parte le cagioni del bene e del male essere loro, e mostro e modi con li quali molti hanno cerco di acquistarli e tenerli, mi resta ora a discorrere generalmente le offese e difese che in ciascuno de' prenominati possono accadere. Noi abbiamo detto di sopra come a uno principe è necessario avere e sua fondamenti buoni, altrimenti, di necessità conviene che ruini. E principali fondamenti che abbino tutti li stati, così nuovi come vecchi o misti, sono le buone legge e le buone arme. E perchè e' non può essere buone legge dove non sono buone arme, e dove sono buone arme conviene sieno buone legge, io lascerò indrieto il ragionare delle legge e parlerò delle arme.

Dico, adunque, che l'arme con le quali uno principe defende il suo stato, o le sono proprie, o le sono mercenarie, o ausiliarie, o miste. Le mercenarie e ausiliarie sono inutile e periculose. E se uno tiene lo stato suo fondato in su le armi mercenarie, non starà mai fermo nè sicuro; perchè le sono disunite, ambiziose, sanza disciplina, infedele; gagliarde fra li amici; fra e nimici, vile; non timore di Dio, non fede con li uomini; e tanto si differisce la ruina, quanto si differisce lo assalto; e nella pace se' spogliato da loro, nella guerra da' nimici. La cagione di questo è che le non hanno altro amore, nè altra cagione che le tenga in campo, che uno poco di stipendio; il quale non è sufficiente a fare che voglino morire per te. Vogliono bene essere tua soldati mentre che tu non fai guerra; ma come la guerra viene, o fuggirsi o andarsene. La qual cosa doverrei durare poca fatica a persuadere, perchè ora la ruina di Italia non è causata da altro che per essere, in

XII   The Different Kinds of Troops and Mercenary Soldiers

Having discussed in particular all those kinds of principalities that I proposed to discuss at the beginning, and
having examined, to some extent, the causes for their
success or failure, and having illustrated the ways by
which many have sought to acquire and hold on to them,
there now remain for me to discuss in general the offense
and defense that can be adopted by each of the previously
mentioned principalities. We said above that it was necessary for a prince to have laid good foundations, otherwise he will inevitably come to ruin. The principal foundations of all states, whether new or old or mixed, consist
of good laws and good armed forces; and since there
cannot be good laws where good armies are lacking, and
where there are good armies there must be good laws,
I shall leave aside the discussion of laws and speak about
armed forces.

Let me say, then, that the armies with which a prince
defends his state consist of either his own people or mercenaries, or auxiliary, or a mixture. The mercenaries and
auxiliaries are useless and dangerous: and if one main-
tains his state by means of mercenary troops, he will
never be strong or safe; for they are disunited, ambitious,
without discipline, unfaithful; they are courageous among
friends; among enemies they are cowards; they have no
fear of God, no faith in other men; and your downfall
is deferred only as long as the attack is deferred; in peace-
time you are plundered by them, in wartime by enemies.
The cause of this is that they have no other love nor
other reason to keep them in the battlefield than a
meager wage, which is not enough to make them want
to die for you. They love being your soldiers while you
are not waging war, but when war breaks out, they either
flee or move away. Of this it would take me little effort

spazio di molti anni, riposatasi in su le arme mercenarie. Le quali feciono già per alcuno qualche progresso, e parevano gagliarde infra loro; ma come venne el forestiero, le mostrorno quello che le erano; onde che a Carlo re di Francia fu licito pigliare la Italia col gesso. E chi diceva come e' n' erano cagione e peccati nostri, diceva el vero; ma non erano già quelli che credeva, ma questi che io ho narrati; e perchè egli erano peccati de' principi, ne hanno patito la pena ancora loro.

Io voglio dimostrare meglio la infelicità di queste arme. E capitani mercenarii, o e' sono uomini nelle armi eccellenti, o no: se sono, non te ne puoi fidare, perchè sempre aspireranno alla grandezza propria, o con lo opprimere te che li se' patrone, o con lo opprimere altri fuora della tua intenzione; ma se non è il capitano virtuoso, e' ti rovina per l' ordinario. E se si responde che qualunque arà arme in mano farà questo, o mercenario o no, replicherei come le arme hanno ad essere operate o da uno principe o da una republica: el principe debbe andare in persona, e fare lui l' offizio del capitano; la republica ha a mandare sua cittadini; e quando ne manda uno che non riesca valente uomo, debbe cambiarlo; e quando e' sia, tenerlo con le leggi, che non passi el segno. E per esperienza si vede a' principi soli e republiche armate fare progressi grandissimi, e alle armi mercenarie non fare mai se non danno; e con più difficultà viene alla obedienzia di uno suo citadino una republica armata di arme proprie, che una armata di armi esterne.

to convince you, for the present ruin of Italy is caused by nothing other than her having depended for a long period of time on mercenary troops. At times they did help some people to get ahead, and they appeared courageous in combat with other mercenaries; but as soon as the foreigner came, they showed themselves for what they were, and so Charles, king of France, was allowed to take Italy with chalk.[1] And he[2] who said that our sins were the cause, said the truth; but they certainly were not the sins he thought, but rather the ones I have just recounted; and since these were the sins of princes, they have come in turn to suffer the penalty for them.

I wish to demonstrate further the unfortunate results of such troops. The mercenary captains are either excellent soldiers or they are not: if they are, you cannot trust them, because they will always aspire to their own greatness either by oppressing you who are master, or by oppressing others whom you had no intention of oppressing; however, if the captain is not skillful, he will as a result ruin you. And if someone were to reply that whoever bears arms will act this way, whether it be a mercenary or not, I would answer that armies should be managed by a prince or by a republic: the prince should appear in person and take the part of captain himself; the republic must send its own citizens; and when they send one who does not prove to be a capable man, they should change him; and if he be capable they should keep him in check by means of the law so that he will not step outside his bounds. And it is seen through experience how only princes and armed republics make enormous progress, and how mercenary troops do nothing if not damage; and a republic armed with its own troops is less likely to fall under the tyranny of a single citizen than one armed with foreign troops.

Stettono Roma e Sparta molti secoli armate e libere. E
Svizzeri sono armatissimi e liberissimi. Delle armi mercenarie antiche in exemplis sono e Cartaginesi; li quali
furono per essere oppressi da' loro soldati mercenarii,
finita la prima guerra con li Romani, ancora che a Cartaginesi avessino, per capi, loro proprii cittadini. Filippo
Macedone fu fatto da' Tebani, dopo la morte di Epami-
nunda, capitano delle loro gente; e tolse loro, dopo la
vittoria, la libertà. E Milanesi, morto il duca Filippo,
soldorno Francesco Sforza contro a' Viniziani; il quale,
superati gli inimici a Caravaggio, si congiunse con loro
per opprimere e Milanesi sua patroni. Sforza, suo padre,
sendo soldato della regina Giovanna di Napoli, la lasciò
in uno tratto disarmata; onde lei, per non perdere el
regno, fu costretta gittarsi in grembo al re di Aragona. E
se Viniziani e Fiorentini hanno per lo adrieto cresciuto
lo imperio loro con queste armi, e li loro capitani non se
ne sono però fatti principi ma gli hanno difesi, respondo
che e Fiorentini in questo caso sono suti favoriti dalla
sorte; perchè de' capitani virtuosi, de' quali potevano
temere, alcuni non hanno vinto, alcuni hanno avuto op-
posizione, altri hanno volto la ambizione loro altrove.
Quello che non vinse fu Giovanni Aucut, del quale, non
vincendo, non si poteva conoscere la fede; ma ognuno
confesserà che, vincendo, stavano e Fiorentini a sua discrezione. Sforza ebbe sempre e Bracceschi contrarii, che
guardorono l'uno l'altro. Francesco volse l'ambizione
sua in Lombardia; Braccio contro alla Chiesa e il regno
di Napoli.

Ma vegnàno a quello che è seguito poco tempo fa.
Feciono e Fiorentini Paulo Vitelli loro capitano, uomo

For many centuries Rome and Sparta stood armed and free. The Swiss are very well armed and very free. An example from antiquity of the use of mercenary troops are the Carthaginians, who, after the first war with the Romans, were nearly overrun by their mercenary soldiers despite the fact that the Carthaginians had their own citizens as leaders. The Thebans, after the death of Epaminondas, made Philip of Macedon[3] captain of their army; and after the victory, he took their freedom from them. The Milanese, after the death of Philip, hired Francesco Sforza to fight against the Venetians; once he had overthrown the enemy at Carvaggio, he joined forces with them in order to oppress the Milanese, his masters. Sforza,[4] his father, while in the pay of queen Giovanna of Naples, all of a sudden left her without troops; whereby in order not to lose the kingdom she was forced to throw herself into the lap of the king of Aragon. And if the Venetians and the Florentines have in the past increased their domain with such troops, and their captains did not as a result set themselves up as princes but rather defended them, my answer is that the Florentines in this case were favored by luck; for among those brave captains that they had reason to fear, some of them did not conquer, some met with opposition, others turned their ambitions elsewhere. The one who did not conquer was John Hawkwood,[5] whose loyalty, since he did not succeed in conquering, cannot be known; but anyone would confess that, had he conquered, the Florentines would have been at his mercy. The Sforzas always had the Bracceschi[6] as opponents, so that they kept a check on each other. Francesco turned his ambitions in the direction of Lombardy; Braccio against the Church[7] and the kingdom of Naples.

But let us come to what has happened just recently. The Florentines chose for their captain Paulo Vitelli, a

prudentissimo, e che, di privata fortuna, aveva presa grandissima reputazione. Se costui espugnava Pisa, veruno fia
che nieghi come conveniva a' Fiorentini stare seco; perchè,
se fussi diventato soldato di loro nimici, non avevano
remedio; e se lo tenevano, aveano a obedirlo. E Viniziani,
se si considerrà e progressi loro, si vedrà quelli avere
securamente e gloriosamente operato mentre ferono la
guerra loro proprii (che fu avanti che si volgessino con le
loro imprese in terra); dove co' gentili uomini e con la
plebe armata operorono virtuosissimamente. Ma come e'
cominciorno a combattere in terra, lasciorno questa virtù
e seguitorno e costumi delle guerre di Italia. E nel principio dello augumento loro in terra, per non vi avere
molto stato e per essere in grande reputazione, non aveano
da temere molto de' loro capitani; ma, come elli amplio-
rono (che fu sotto el Carmignuola), ebbono uno saggio
di questo errore; perchè, vedutolo virtuosissimo, battuto
che loro ebbono sotto il suo governo el duca di Milano,
e conoscendo dall'altra parte come egli era raffreddo
nella guerra, iudicorono non potere con lui più vincere
perchè non voleva, nè potere licenziarlo, per non riperdere
ciò che aveano acquistato; onde che furono necessitati,
per assicurarsene, ammazzarlo. Hanno di poi avuto per
loro capitani Bartolomeo da Bergamo, Ruberto da San
Severino, Conte di Pitigliano, e simili; con e quali aveano
a temere della perdita, non del guadagno loro: come
intervenne di poi a Vailà, dove, in una giornata, perderono
quello che in ottocento anni, con tanta fatica, avevano
acquistato. Perchè da queste armi nascono solo e lenti,
tardi e deboli acquisti, e le sùbite e miraculose perdite.
E perchè io sono venuto, con questi esempli, in Italia, la
quale è stata molti anni governata dalle arme mercenarie,
le voglio discorrere più da alto, acciò che, veduto la origine
e progressi di esse, si possa meglio correggerle.

since my examples all deal with Italy, which has been for many years under the command of mercenary troops, I want to go into this more deeply, so that their origin and line of development having been observed, they can be more easily corrected.

You must understand then, how in recent times, as soon as the empire began to be rejected by Italy and the Pope began to gain more prestige in temporal matters, Italy was broken up into more states; for many of the large cities took up arms against their nobles who, formerly backed by the Emperor, had kept them oppressed; and the Church supported these uprisings to increase its temporal power; their citizens became princes in many other cities. Whereby, Italy having arrived at the stage of being almost entirely in the hands of the Church and a few republics, those priests and other citizens having no knowledge in the use of arms began to hire foreigners. The first to give prestige to such troops was Alberigo of Conio,[12] a Romagnol. From his school of thought came, among others, Braccio and Sforza, who in their times were the arbiters of Italy. After them came all the others who until our own times have commanded these troops. And the effect of their ingenuity has been that Italy has been overrun by Charles, preyed upon by Louis, humiliated by Ferdinand and insulted by the Swiss. Their procedure was first to enhance their own prestige by detracting from that of the infantry. They did this because they were men without a state of their own who lived by their profession, and just a few foot soldiers would give them no prestige, and they could not support a large number of them; and so they limited themselves to horsemen, and since there was a reasonable number of them they were provided for and honored. And they worked things out to the point that in an army of twenty thousand soldiers the number of foot soldiers did not reach

traevano la notte alle terre; quelli della terra non traevano alle tende; non facevano intorno al campo nè steccato nè fossa; non campeggiavano el verno. E tutte queste cose erano permesse ne' loro ordini militari, e trovate da loro per fuggire, come è detto, e la fatica e gli pericoli: tanto che gli hanno condotta Italia stiava e vituperata.

NOTES

1. This expression comes from a statement that Philippe de Commynes attributes to Pope Alexander vi in reference to the facility with which Charles' army managed to come through Italy to Naples in 1494–5.

2. Savonarola.

3. The example of Philip of Macedon (father of Alexander the Great) seems to be a weak one, because Philip was not actually a *condottiere* but only an ally of the Thessalians and the Thebans against the Focesi in the so-called Sacred War (355–53 B.C.).

4. *Sforza his father*. Muzio Attendolo, Francesco's father, was a great *condottiere* in the pay of Ladislaus, the King of Naples, and then of Giovanna ii, the King's successor, until 1426 when he abandoned her to pass into the service of Louis xiii of Anjou, claimant to the throne.

5. John Hawkwood, the English condottiere who came into Italy in 1361, was a famous captain at the service of the Florentines from 1377 until his death in 1393.

6. The Bracceschi, commanded first by Braccio da Montone and then by Niccolò Piccinino and Niccolò Fortebraccio, competed in 1400 with the Sforzeschi who had as leader first Muzio Attendolo and then Francesco Sforza.

7. Before passing into the hire of Queen Giovanna of Naples, Braccio da Montone had been in the service of Gio-

two thousand. They had, besides this, used every means to spare both themselves and their soldiers any hardships and fear, not killing one another in battle but rather taking prisoners and not asking ransom. They would not attack a town at night; and those in the town would not attack the tents; they constructed neither stockades nor trenches around the campsite; they did not wage war in winter. And all these things were permitted by their military code and provided them the means to escape, as was said, hardships and dangers: so that they have led Italy into slavery and degradation.

vanni XXIII, during whose absence he had occupied the cities of Perugia, Assisi, and Todi. After the return of the pontificate from the Council of Constance, he was set against Sforza, who conquered and killed him in 1424.

8. Carmagnola, Francesco Bussone, Count of Carmagnola, was one of the most courageous "soldiers of fortune" of the time. He passed from the service of F. M. Visconti to that of the Venetians in 1425. He conquered the Milanese at Maclodio on October 12, 1427; however, having procrastinated in his move against Francesco Sforza and Niccolò Piccinino, he was suspected of connivance with the Visconti and was tried and condemned to death in 1432.

9. Bartolomeo Colleoni da Bergamo (1400–1475) was first in the hire of the Venetians, and he was defeated by F. Sforza in 1448 at Caravaggio; he was hired by Sforza, only to return later to the service of the Venetians once again.

10. Roberto da San Severino was at the service of the Florentines, then was captain of the Venetians during the war against Ferrara (1482–1484).

11. Niccolò Orsini (1442–1510), Count of Pitigliano, was also hired by the Venetians and was commander of their army in the battle of Vailà.

12. Alberigo da Barbiano, Count of Conio, founded the "Company of St. George," the first Italian mercenary company. He died in 1409.

L'armi ausiliarie, che sono l'altre armi inutili, sono quando si chiama uno potente che con le armi sue ti venga ad aiutare e defendere; come fece ne' prossimi tempi papa Iulio; il quale, avendo visto nella impresa di Ferrara la trista pruova delle sue armi mercenarie, si volse alle ausiliarie, e convenne con Ferrando re di Spagna che con le sue gente ed eserciti dovessi aiutarlo. Queste arme possono essere utile e buone per loro medesime, ma sono, per chi le chiama, quasi sempre dannose; perchè, perdendo, rimani disfatto: vincendo, resti loro prigione. E ancora che di questi esempli ne sieno piene le antiche istorie, non di manco io non mi voglio partire da questo esemplo fresco di papa Iulio II; il partito del quale non potè essere manco considerato: per volere Ferrara, cacciarsi tutto nelle mani d'uno forestiere. Ma la sua buona fortuna fece nascere una terza cosa, acciò non cogliessi el frutto della sua mala elezione: perchè, sendo li ausiliarii sua rotti a Ravenna, e surgendo e Svizzeri, che cacciorno e vincitori fuora di ogni opinione e sua e d'altri, venne a non rimanere prigione delli inimici, sendo fugati, nè delli ausiliarii sua, avendo vinto con altre armi che con le loro. E Fiorentini, sendo al tutto disarmati, condussono diecimila Franzesi a Pisa per espugnarla; per il quale partito portorono più pericolo che in qualunque tempo de' travagli loro. Lo imperadore di Costantinopoli, per opporsi alli sua vicini, misse in Grecia diecimila Turchi; li quali, finita la guerra, non se ne volsero partire; il che fu principio della servitù di Grecia con gli infedeli.

Colui, adunque, che vuole non potere vincere, si vaglia di queste arme, perchè sono molto più pericolose che le

XIII   On Auxiliary, Mixed and Native Troops

Auxiliary troops, the other kind of useless armies, are those that come when you call a powerful person and his soldiers to your aid and defense: as was done in recent times by Pope Julius who, having observed the sad trial of his mercenary troops in the battle of Ferrara, turned to auxiliary troops and agreed with Ferdinand, king of Spain, that he aid him with his soldiers and armies.[1] These troops can be useful and good in themselves, but for the one who calls on them they are almost always harmful or dangerous; for, if they lose, you remain defeated; if they win, you end up their prisoner. And though ancient history is full of such cases, I nonetheless do not want to depart from this recent case concerning Pope Julius II, whose plan of action could not have been more thoughtless, for in wanting to have Ferrara he threw himself entirely into the hands of a foreigner. But his good fortune gave rise to a third factor, which prevented him from reaping the fruits of his bad choice: for, when his auxiliaries were beaten at Ravenna, the Swiss swept down, and to the surprise of Julius as well as everyone else, drove out the victors, and as a result he was neither taken prisoner by his enemies, for they had fled, nor by his auxiliaries, for he was victorious by means of other arms and not theirs. The Florentines, having absolutely no arms of their own, hired ten thousand Frenchmen to seize Pisa; such a move put them in more danger than any of their previous trials. The emperor of Constantinople,[2] in order to oppose his neighboring powers, brought into Greece ten thousand Turkish soldiers who, once the war was over, did not want to leave; this was the beginning of the Greek slavery under the infidel.

Let him, therefore, who desires not to be able to win make use of these troops; for they are much more

mercenarie. Perchè in queste è la ruina fatta: sono tutte unite, tutte volte alla obedienzia di altri; ma nelle mercenarie, a offenderti, vinto che le hanno, bisogna più tempo e maggiore occasione, non sendo tutto uno corpo, ed essendo trovate e pagate da te; nelle quali uno terzo che tu facci capo, non può pigliare subito tanta autorità che ti offenda. In somma, nelle mercenarie è più pericolosa la ignavia, nelle ausiliarie, la virtù.

Uno principe, pertanto, savio sempre ha fuggito queste arme e voltosi alle proprie; e ha volsuto piuttosto perdere con li sua che vincere con gli altri, iudicando non vera vittoria quella che con le armi aliene si acquistassi. Io non dubiterò mai di allegare Cesare Borgia e le sue azioni. Questo duca entrò in Romagna con le armi ausiliarie, conducendovi tutte gente franzese; e con quelle prese Imola e Furlì. Ma non li parendo poi tale arme secure, si volse alle mercenarie, iudicando in quelle manco periculo, e soldò li Orsini e Vitelli. Le quali poi nel maneggiare trovando dubbie e infedeli e periculose, le spense, e volsesi alle proprie. E puossi facilmente vedere che differenzia è infra l'una e l'altra di queste arme, considerato che differenzia fu dalla reputazione del duca, quando aveva e Franzesi soli e quando aveva li Orsini e Vitelli, a quando e' rimase con li soldati suoi e sopra se stesso: e sempre si troverrà accresciuta; nè mai fu stimato assai, se non quando ciascuno vidde che lui era intero possessore delle sue armi.

Io non mi volevo partire dalli esempli italiani e freschi; tamen non voglio lasciare indrieto Ierone Siracusano, sendo

dangerous than mercenaries. With them lies sure defeat: they are all united, all resolved to the obedience of others; but the mercenaries, though they may have been victorious, in order to do you any harm they must have more time and a better opportunity; for existing as a disunited body of men hired and paid by you, a third party whom you may put in charge of them cannot immediately seize enough authority to harm you. And so, with mercenaries, the most dangerous thing is their cowardice; with auxiliaries, their courage.

A prince who is wise, then, has always avoided these troops and turned to his own, and he has chosen rather to lose with his own troops than win with those of others, having decided that a victory achieved by means of foreign armies is not a real one. I shall not hesitate to cite as an example Cesare Borgia and his actions. This duke entered Romagna with auxiliary troops, leading a group composed entirely of Frenchmen, and with them he captured Imola and Forlì; but then, when they no longer seemed to him trustworthy, he turned to mercenaries, deciding there would be less danger in using them; and he hired the Orsini and the Vitelli; once he discovered they were unreliable, disloyal, and treacherous in his service, he did away with them and turned to his own men. And it is easy to see the difference between these two kinds of troops, after having examined the difference between the duke's prestige when he had only Frenchmen and when he had the Orsini and Vitelli, and when he was left with his own soldiers and himself to depend on: and we find his prestige continuously growing; never was he so highly esteemed than when everyone came to see that he was absolute master of his own troops.

I did not want to depart from using recent Italian examples; nevertheless, I do not want to omit Hiero of

uno de' sopranominati da me. Costui, come io dissi, fatto
da' Siracusani capo delli eserciti, conobbe subito quella
milizia mercenaria non essere utile, per essere condottieri
fatti come li nostri italiani; e parendoli non li potere
tenere nè lasciare, li fece tutti tagliare a pezzi: e di poi
fece guerra con le arme sua e non con le aliene. Voglio
ancora ridurre a memoria una figura del Testamento
Vecchio fatta a questo proposito. Offerendosi David a
Saul di andare a combattere con Golia, provocatore fili-
steo, Saul, per darli animo, l'armò delle arme sua; le
quali come David ebbe indosso, recusò, dicendo con
quelle non si potere bene valere di se stesso; e però voleva
trovare el nimico con la sua fromba e con il suo coltello.

In fine, l'arme d'altri, o le ti caggiono di dosso, o le ti
pesano, o le ti stringono. Carlo VII, padre del re Luigi XI,
avendo, con la sua fortuna e virtù, libera Francia dalli
Inghilesi, conobbe questa necessità di armarsi di arme
proprie, e ordinò nel suo regno l'ordinanza delle gente
d'arme e delle fanterie. Di poi il re Luigi, suo figliuolo,
spense quella de' fanti e cominciò a soldare Svizzeri; il
quale errore, seguitato dagli altri, è, come si vede ora in
fatto, cagione de' pericoli di quello regno. Perchè, avendo
dato reputazione a' Svizzeri, ha invilito tutte le arme sua;
perchè le fanterie ha spento in tutto e le sua gente d'arme
ha obligato alle arme d'altri; perchè, sendo assuefatte a
militare con Svizzeri, non pare loro di potere vincere
sanza essi. Di qui nasce che Franzesi contro a Svizzeri
non bastano, e sanza Svizzeri contro ad altri non pruo-
vono. Sono, dunque, stati li eserciti di Francia misti, parte
mercenarii e parte proprii; le quali armi tutte insieme
sono molto migliori che le semplici ausiliarie o le semplici

Syracuse, whom I have mentioned previously. This man, as I said before, having been made head of the armed forces by the Syracusans, realized immediately that mercenary troops, resembling our own Italian *condottieri*, were useless; and it seemed to him that he could neither keep them nor dismiss them, so he had them all cut into pieces: and from then on he waged war with his own troops and not with those of others. I would also like to recall to mind an example from the Old Testament suitable for this argument. When David offered himself to Saul to go and fight against Goliath, the Philistine troublemaker, Saul, in order to encourage him, armed him with his own arms, which David, once he had them on, cast off, saying that with them he could not prove his true worth, and that he wished rather to meet the enemy with his own sling and his own sword.

In other words, someone else's arms either slip off our back or they are too heavy or too light for us. Charles VII,[3] father of Louis XI,[4] having, by means of his good fortune and his ingenuity, liberated France from the English, recognized this necessity of arming oneself with one's own arms, and he set up an ordinance in his kingdom to provide for horsemen and foot soldiers. Later on King Louis, his son, abolished the ordinance for foot soldiers and began to hire the Swiss; which error, followed by others, is as we now in fact can see the cause of the dangers in that kingdom. By having given prestige to the Swiss, he degraded all his own troops; for he did away entirely with his foot soldiers and put his horsemen in the service of others; and having grown accustomed to fighting with the Swiss, they came to feel they could not win without them; from this it follows that the French are not strong enough to oppose the Swiss, and, without the Swiss, they would not attempt to oppose anyone else. The armies of

mercenarie, e molto inferiore alle proprie. E basti lo esemplo detto; perchè el regno di Francia sarebbe insuperabile, se l' ordine di Carlo era accresciuto o perservato. Ma la poca prudenzia delli uomini comincia una cosa che, per sapere allora di buono, non si accorge del veleno che vi è sotto; come io dissi, di sopra, delle febbre etiche.

Pertanto colui che in uno principato non conosce e mali quando nascono, non è veramente savio; e questo è dato a pochi. E se si considerassi la prima cagione della ruina dello imperio romano, si troverrà essere suto solo cominciare a soldare e Goti; perchè da quello principio cominciorno a enervare le forze dello imperio romano; e tutta quella virtù che si levava da lui, si dava a loro.

Concludo, adunque, che, sanza avere arme proprie, nessuno principato è securo; anzi è tutto obligato alla fortuna, non avendo virtù che nelle avversità con fede lo difenda. E fu sempre opinione e sentenzia delli uomini savii « quod nihil sit tam infirmum aut instabile quam fama potentiae non sua vi nixa ». E l' arme proprie son quelle che sono composte o di sudditi o di cittadini o di creati tua; tutte l' altre sono o mercenarie o ausiliarie. E il modo a ordinare l' arme proprie sarà facile a trovare, se si discorrerà gli ordini de' quattro sopra nominati da me, e se si vedrà come Filippo, padre di Alessandro Magno, e come molte repubbliche e principi si sono armati e ordinati; a' quali ordini io al tutto mi rimetto.

France, then, have been mixed, in part mercenary and in part their own: armies joined together in this way are far superior to those that are strictly auxiliary or strictly mercenary, and greatly inferior to one's own native troops. And this example should be enough, because the kingdom of France would have been insuperable if the ordinance of Charles had been developed or preserved. But man's little foresight will initiate a project which at the start seems good, but it does not notice the poison that is underlying it: as I said previously in regard to consumptive fevers.[5]

And so whoever does not recognize evils when they arise in a principality is not truly wise; and this ability is given to only a few. And if we examine the primary cause of the downfall of the Roman Empire, we will find that it was only when the Goths began to be hired as mercenaries that the strength of the Roman Empire began to weaken, and all that power which was drained from it went to them.

I conclude, then, that without having one's own native troops, no principality is secure and is entirely subjected to fortune, not having the power and the loyalty to defend it in bad times. It has always been the contention and judgment of wise men "that nothing is so unhealthy and unstable as a reputation for power that is not founded on one's own."[6] And one's own arms are those that are made up either of subjects or citizens or your own dependents: all the rest are either mercenaries or auxiliaries. And the way to organize a native army is easily found, if you examine the methods followed by those four men I mentioned above, and take note of how Philip, father of Alexander the Great, and how numerous republics and princes have armed and organized themselves: in such methods as theirs I have complete confidence.

NOTES

1. Bologna having been occupied, Pope Julius II wanted to seize Ferrara as well (1510). However, when it was conquered by Alfonso d'Este and the French army, he not only had to give up that enterprise, but was forced to leave Bologna. He then formed a military alliance with the King of Spain (Lega Santa, 1511).

2. Emperor of Constantinople, John Cantacuzene, in his struggle against the Paleologhi, enlisted an army of ten thousand Turks commanded by Soliman, the Sultan's son.

3. Charles VII (1422–1461), the King of France, ended the Hundred Years' War (1337–1461) against the English victoriously for France. During the truce from 1435–1436 he created the French civic army, the "companies of ordinance."

4. Louis XI (1461–1483), the real and great reorganizer of the French monarchy, hired Swiss soldiers in 1474, abolishing the established ordinance.

5. A reference to his discussion of disease in Chapter III.

6. Machiavelli was probably thinking of a phrase by Tacitus (*Annals*, XIII, 19): *"nihil rerum mortalium tam instabile ac fluxum est quam fama potentiae non sua vi nixae."*

Debbe, adunque, uno principe non avere altro obietto, nè altro pensiero, nè prendere cosa alcuna per sua arte, fuora della guerra e ordini e disciplina di essa; perchè quella è sola arte che si espetta a chi comanda; ed è di tanta virtù che non solamente mantiene quelli che sono nati principi, ma molte volte fa li uomini di privata fortuna salire a quel grado; e, per adverso, si vede che quando e principi hanno pensato più alle delicatezze che alle armi, hanno perso lo stato loro. E la prima cagione che ti fa perdere quello, è negligere questa arte; e la cagione che te lo fa acquistare, è lo essere professo di questa arte.

Francesco Sforza, per essere armato, di privato diventò duca di Milano; e figliuoli, per fuggire e disagi delle arme, di duchi diventorono privati. Perchè, intra le altre cagioni che ti arreca di male, lo essere disarmato ti fa contennendo; la quale è una di quelle infamie dalle quali el principe si debbe guardare, come di sotto si dirà: perchè da uno armato a uno disarmato non è proporzione alcuna; e non è ragionevole che chi è armato obedisca volentieri a chi è disarmato, e che il disarmato stia securo intra servitori armati; perchè, sendo nell'uno sdegno e nell'altro sospetto, non è possibile operino bene insieme. E però uno principe che della milizia non si intenda, oltre alle altre infelicità, come è detto, non può essere stimato da' sua soldati, nè fidarsi di loro.

Debbe, pertanto, mai levare il pensiero da questo eser- cizio della guerra, e nella pace vi si debbe più esercitare che nella guerra; il che può fare in dua modi; l'uno con le opere, l'altro con la mente. E quanto alle opere, oltre al tenere bene ordinati ed esercitati e sua, debbe stare sempre in su le cacce, e mediante quelle assuefare el

XIV What a Prince Should Do with Regard to the Militia

A prince, therefore, should have no other goal or thought, nor should he make anything his major concern, but war, its organization and discipline, because that is the only concern that awaits one who rules; and it is of such efficacy that not only does it sustain those who were born princes, but many times it will cause a man to rise from private life to that level; and, to the contrary, it is clear that once princes have given more thought to personal pleasures than to arms, they have lost their domain. And the first way to lose it is to neglect this art; and the way to acquire it is to be well prepared in this art.

Francesco Sforza, because he was armed, from a private citizen became duke of Milan; his successors, because they fled the inconveniences of arms, from dukes became private citizens. For, among the other bad results that being disarmed brings about, it makes you despicable: one of those infamies a prince should guard against, as will be discussed below; for there is no comparison whatsoever between an armed and an unarmed man, and it is not reasonable to expect one who is armed to obey willingly one who is unarmed, and that an unarmed person will be safe in the midst of his armed servants; for, with the latter being scornful, and the former suspicious, it is impossible for them to work well together. And so a prince who has no comprehension of military affairs, among the other misfortunes already mentioned, cannot be respected by his soldiers nor can he trust them.

Therefore, he should never lift his thought from the pursuit of war; he should pursue it even more in time of peace than in time of war, which can be done in two ways: one by action, the other by the mind. And as far as actions are concerned, besides maintaining his men well disciplined and trained, he should always be out

corpo a' disagi; e parte imparare la natura de' siti, e conoscere come surgono e monti, come imboccono le valle,
come iacciono e piani, ed intendere la natura de' fiumi e
de' paduli; e in questo porre grandissima cura. La quale
cognizione è utile in dua modi; prima, si impara a conoscere el suo paese e può meglio intendere le difese di
esso; di poi, mediante la cognizione e pratica di quelli
siti, con facilità comprendere ogni altro sito che di nuovo
li sia necessario speculare; perchè li poggi, le valle, e
piani, e fiumi, e paduli che sono, verbigrazia, in Toscana,
hanno con quelli delle altre provincie certa similitudine;
tale che, dalla cognizione del sito di una provincia, si
può facilmente venire alla cognizione dell'altre. E quel
principe che manca di questa perizia, manca della prima
parte che vuole avere uno capitano; perchè, questa, insegna trovare el nimico, pigliare li alloggiamenti, condurre
li eserciti, ordinare le giornate, campeggiare le terre con
tuo vantaggio.

Filipomene, principe delli Achei, intra le altre laude
che dalli scrittori li sono date, è che ne' tempi della pace
non pensava mai se non a' modi della guerra; e quando
era in campagna con gli amici, spesso si fermava e ragio-
nava con quelli: «Se li nimici fussino in su quel colle, e
noi ci trovassimo qui col nostro esercito, chi di noi arebbe
vantaggio? come si potrebbe ire, servando li ordini, a
trovarli? se noi volessimo ritirarci, come aremmo a fare?
se loro si ritirassino, come aremmo a seguirli?» e propo-
neva loro, andando, tutti e casi che in uno esercito possino occorrere; intendeva la opinione loro, diceva la sua,
corroboravala con le ragioni; tal che, per queste continue
cogitazioni, non posseva mai, guidando gli eserciti, nascere
accidente alcuno che lui non avessi el remedio.

hunting, and in so doing accustom his body to hardships; and at the same time learn the layout of the terrain, and know how mountains slope, how valleys open, how plains lie, and understand the nature of rivers and marshes; and to these things he should devote a great deal of attention. Such knowledge is useful in two ways: first, one learns to know his own country, and he can better understand how to defend it; then, with his knowledge of and experience with the terrain, he can grasp easily the layout of any other terrain he may find necessary to explore for the first time. For the hills, valleys, plains, the rivers and marshes that are, for instance, in Tuscany, have certain features in common with those of other provinces; so that, from knowing how the terrain is laid out in one province, one can easily arrive at an understanding of it in others. And that prince who lacks this skill lacks the principal quality necessary in a captain, because such skill teaches you how to locate the enemy, choose a campsite, lead the troops, set them up for battle, besiege cities to your own advantage.

Philopoemen,[1] prince of the Achaeans, among the other praises that writers have bestowed on him, is praised because in time of peace he thought of nothing except the ways of making war; and when he was out in the country with his friends, he would often stop and debate with them: "If the enemy were on top of that hill, and we found ourselves here with an army, which of us would have the advantage? How could we advance to meet them without breaking ranks? If we wished to retreat, how would we do it? If they were to retreat, how would we go after them?" and he brought up to them, as they went along, every predicament an army may find itself in; he would listen to their opinions, he would express his own, supporting it with reasons; so that, because of this con-

Ma quanto allo esercizio della mente, debbe il principe leggere le istorie, e in quelle considerare le azioni delli uomini eccellenti; vedere come si sono governati nelle guerre; esaminare le cagioni delle vittorie e perdite loro, per potere queste fuggire e quelle imitare; e sopratutto fare come ha fatto per lo adrieto qualche uomo eccellente, che ha preso a imitare se alcuno innanzi a lui è stato laudato e gloriato, e di quello ha tenuto sempre e gesti e azioni appresso di sè: come si dice che Alessandro Magno imitava Achille; Cesare, Alessandro; Scipione, Ciro. E qualunque legge la vita di Ciro scritta da Senofonte, riconosce di poi, nella vita di Scipione, quanto quella imitazione gli fu di gloria, e quanto, nella castità, affabilità, umanità, liberalità, Scipione si conformassi con quelle cose che di Ciro da Senofonte sono sute scritte.

Questi simili modi debbe osservare uno principe savio; e mai ne' tempi pacifici stare ozioso; ma con industria farne capitale, per potersene valere nelle avversità, acciò che, quando si muta la fortuna, lo truovi parato a resisterle.

stant meditation, when leading his troops no possible incident could arise for which he did not have the solution.

But as for the exercise of the mind, the prince should read history, and in it study the actions of distinguished men; to see how they comported themselves in war; to examine the causes for their victories and defeats in order to be able to avoid the latter and imitate the former; and above all he should do as some outstanding man before him has done, who decided to imitate someone who has been praised and honored before him and always keep in mind his deeds and actions: just as it is said that Alexander the Great imitated Achilles; Caesar, Alexander; Scipio, Cyrus. And whoever reads the life of Cyrus written by Xenophon,[2] then realizes how important in the life of Scipio that imitation was to his glory, and how much, in purity, affability, kindness, generosity, Scipio conformed to those qualities of Cyrus that Xenophon has written about.

Such methods as these a wise prince should observe, and never remain idle during peaceful times, but zealously turn them into gain that will show profit during adverse times, so that, when fortune changes, it will find him ready to resist such times.

NOTES

1. Philopoemen (253–183 B.C.) was the head and most able strategist of the Achaean League.

2. Xenophon, the Greek writer (445–335 B.C.), was author of numerous writings of historic and political character, among them the "Ciropedia" (*Education of Cyrus*).

XV De His Rebus Quibus Homines et Praesertim Principes Laudantur aut Vituperantur

Resta ora a vedere quali debbano essere e modi e governi di uno principe con sudditi o con li amici. E perchè io so che molti di questo hanno scritto, dubito, scrivendone ancora io, non essere tenuto prosuntuoso, partendomi massime, nel disputare questa materia, dalli ordini delli altri. Ma sendo l'intento mio scrivere cosa utile a chi la intende, mi è parso più conveniente andare drieto alla verità effettuale della cosa, che alla imaginazione di essa. E molti si sono imaginati republiche e principati che non si sono mai visti nè conosciuti essere in vero; perchè egli è tanto discosto da come si vive a come si doverrebbe vivere, che colui che lascia quello che si fa per quello che si doverrebbe fare impara piuttosto la ruina che la perservazione sua; perchè uno uomo che voglia fare in tutte le parte professione di buono, conviene ruini infra tanti che non sono buoni. Onde è necessario a uno principe, volendosi mantenere, imparare a potere essere non buono, e usarlo e non l'usare secondo la necessità.

Lasciando, adunque, indrieto le cose circa uno principe imaginate, e discorrendo quelle che sono vere, dico che tutti li uomini, quando se ne parla, e massime e principi, per essere posti più alti, sono notati di alcune di queste qualità che arrecano loro o biasimo o laude. E questo è che alcuno è tenuto liberale, alcuno misero (usando uno termine toscano, perchè avaro in nostra lingua è ancora colui che per rapina desidera di avere; misero chiamiamo noi quello che si astiene troppo di usare il suo); alcuno è tenuto donatore, alcuno rapace; alcuno crudele, alcuno pietoso; l'uno fedifrago, l'altro fedele; l'uno effeminato e pusillanime, l'altro feroce e animoso; l'uno umano, l'altro superbo; l'uno lascivo, l'altro casto;

XV On Those Things for Which Men, and Especially Princes, Are Praised or Blamed

Now there remains to be seen what ought to be the criteria and actions of a prince in dealing with his subjects and friends. And because I know that many have written about this, I am afraid, by writing about it again, that I shall be thought presumptuous, all the more so for departing, in my discussion of this material, from the procedures of others. But my intention being to write something useful for whoever understands it, it seemed to me more appropriate to pursue the effectual truth of the matter rather than its imagined one. And many have imagined republics and principalities that have never been seen or known to exist in reality; for there is such a gap between how one lives and how one should live that he who neglects what is being done for what should be done will learn his destruction rather than his preservation: for a man who wishes to profess goodness at all times must fall to ruin among so many who are not good. Whereby it is necessary for a prince who wishes to maintain his position to learn how not to be good, and to use it or not according to necessity.

Putting aside, then, the imagined things concerning a prince, and taking into account those that are true, let me say that all men, when they are spoken of, and especially princes, since they are on a higher level, are judged by some of these qualities which bring them blame or praise. And this is why some are considered to be generous, others stingy (using a Tuscan word, since "avaricious" in our language is still used to refer to one whose desire involves robbing others; we call "stingy" that one who over-refrains from using what he has); some are considered givers, others graspers, some cruel, others merciful; one treacherous, another faithful; one effeminate and cowardly, another vigorous and courageous; one friendly,

l'uno intero, l'altro astuto; l'uno duro, l'altro facile; l'uno grave, l'altro leggieri; l'uno religioso, l'altro incredulo, e simili. E io so che ciascuno confesserà che sarebbe laudabilissima cosa in uno principe trovarsi, di tutte le soprascritte qualità, quelle che sono tenute buone; ma perchè le non si possono avere nè interamente osservare, per le condizione umane che non lo consentono, gli è necessario essere tanto prudente che sappi fuggire l'infamia di quelli vizii che li torrebbano lo stato, e da quelli che non gnene tolgano, guardarsi, se gli è possibile; ma non possendo, vi si può con meno respetto lasciare andare. Et etiam non si curi di incorrere nella infamia di quelli vizii sanza quali e' possa difficilmente salvare lo stato; perchè, se si considerrà bene tutto, si troverrà qualche cosa che parrà virtù, e, seguendola, sarebbe la ruina sua; e qualcuna altra che parrà vizio, e, seguendola, ne riesce la securtà e il bene essere suo.

another haughty; one man lascivious, another pure; one sincere, another cunning; one severe, another lenient; one man serious-minded, another frivolous; one religious, another unbelieving, and the like. And I know everyone will agree that it would be a very praiseworthy thing to find in a prince all of the qualities mentioned above that are considered good; but since it is impossible to have and observe all of them, for human nature does not allow it, the prince must be prudent enough to know how to escape the infamy of those vices that would lose him his state, and be on his guard against those that will not lose it for him, if this be possible; but if it prove impossible, he need not be too troubled about foregoing them. And furthermore, he must not be concerned with incurring the infamy of those vices without which it would be difficult to save his state; because taking all carefully into account, he will discover that something that appears to be a virtue, if pursued, will result in his ruin; while some other thing that appears to be a vice, if pursued, will bring about his security and well-being.

Cominciandomi, adunque, alle prime soprascritte qualità, dico come sarebbe bene essere tenuto liberale; nondimanco la liberalità, usata in modo che tu sia tenuto, ti offende; perchè se la si usa virtuosamente e come la si debbe usare, la non fia conosciuta, e non ti cascherà la infamia del suo contrario. E però, a volersi mantenere infra gli uomini el nome del liberale, è necessario non lasciare indrieto alcuna qualità di suntuosità; talmente che sempre uno principe così fatto consumerà in simile opere tutte le sua facultà, e sarà necessitato alla fine, se vi vorrà mantenere el nome del liberale, gravare e populi estraordinariamente ed essere fiscale, e fare tutte quelle cose che si possano fare per avere danari. Il che comincerà a farlo odioso con sudditi, e poco stimare da nessuno, diventando povero; in modo che, con questa sua liberalità avendo offeso li assai e premiato e pochi, sente ogni primo disagio, e periclita in qualunque primo periculo; il che conoscendo lui, e volendosene ritrarre, incorre subito nella infamia del misero.

Uno principe, adunque, non potendo usare questa virtù del liberale, sanza suo danno, in modo che la sia conosciuta, debbe, s' elli è prudente, non si curare del nome del misero; perchè col tempo sarà tenuto sempre più liberale, veggendo che, con la sua parsimonia, le sua entrate li bastano, può defendersi da chi li fa guerra, può fare imprese sanza gravare e populi; talmente che viene a usare liberalità a tutti quelli a chi e' non toglie, che sono infiniti, e miseria a tutti coloro a chi e' non dà, che sono pochi. Ne' nostri tempi noi non abbiamo veduto fare gran cose se non a quelli che sono stati tenuti miseri; gli altri essere spenti. Papa Iulio II, come si fu servito del nome del liberale per aggiugnere al papato, non pensò poi a

XVI   On Generosity and Parsimony

Beginning, then, with the first of the qualities mentioned above I say that it would be good to be thought of as generous; however, generosity employed in such a way as to give you a reputation for it harms you; yet if it is employed virtuously, and as one should employ it, it may not be recognized and you will not escape the infamy of its opposite. And so, if a man wishes to continue to be known among men as generous, he must not neglect any possible means of lavish display; so that a prince of this type will inevitably consume in such displays all his riches, and eventually it will become necessary for him, if he wishes to maintain his reputation for generosity, to burden the people with exaggerated taxes and to do everything possible to get money. This will begin to make him hateful to his subjects, and in becoming poor, he will be respected by no one; so that, as a result of his generosity, having offended the many and rewarded the few, he will feel the effects of any slight disturbance and is likely to fall at the slightest sign of danger; realizing this and wishing to change his ways, he immediately incurs the infamy of the miser.

A prince, therefore, unable to employ this virtue of generosity in a way that will make him known for it without endangering himself, should, if he is wise, not worry about being known as a miser; because with time he will come to be thought of as more and more generous, once the people see that because of his parsimony he finds his revenues are sufficient, he is able to defend himself from whoever wages war against them, he can carry on a campaign without burdening the people; so that he comes to be generous with all those from whom he takes nothing, and they are innumerable, and miserly with all those to whom he gives nothing, and they are few. In our own times we have not seen

mantenerselo, per potere fare guerra; el re di Francia presente ha fatto tante guerre sanza porre uno dazio estraordinario a' suoi, solum perchè alle superflue spese ha sumministrato la lunga parsimonia sua; el re di Spagna presente, se fussi tenuto liberale, non arebbe fatto nè vinto tante imprese.

Pertanto, uno principe debbe esistimare poco, per non avere a rubare e suddi, per potere difendersi, per non diventare povero e contennendo, per non essere forzato di diventare rapace, di incorrere nel nome del misero; perchè questo è uno di quelli vizii che lo fanno regnare. E se alcuno dicessi: Cesare con la liberalità pervenne allo imperio, e molti altri, per essere stati ed essere tenuti liberali, sono venuti a gradi grandissimi; respondo: o tu se' principe fatto, o tu se' in via di acquistarlo; nel primo caso, questa liberalità è dannosa; nel secondo, è bene necessario essere tenuto liberale. E Cesare era uno di quelli che voleva pervenire al principato di Roma; ma se, poi che vi fu venuto, fussi sopravvissuto e non si fussi temperato da quelle spese, arebbe destrutto quello imperio. E se alcuno replicassi: molti sono stati principi, e con li eserciti hanno fatto gran cose, che sono stati tenuti liberalissimi; ti respondo: o el principe spende del suo e de' sua suddi, o di quello d'altri; nel primo caso, debbe essere parco; nell'altro, non debbe lasciare indrieto parte alcuna di liberalità. E quel principe che va con li eserciti, che si pasce di prede, di sacchi e di taglie, maneggia quello di altri, gli è necessaria questa liberalità; altrimenti, non sarebbe seguito da' soldati. E di quello che non è tuo, o di suddi tua, si può essere più largo donatore, come fu

great things accomplished by anyone who was not considered a miser; the others were destroyed. Pope Julius II, though he did make use of his reputation for generosity in order to attain the papacy, decided then not to maintain it in order that he might be able to wage war; the present king of France[1] waged many wars without imposing extra taxes on his people, because his long-practiced parsimony alone provided for his extra expenses; the present king of Spain, had he been considered generous, would not have carried on or won as many campaigns as he did.

Therefore a prince, in order not to have to despoil his subjects, to be able to defend himself, not to become poor and despised, not to be forced into becoming rapacious, should not be too concerned with incurring the name of miser; because it is one of those vices that allows him to reign. And if someone were to say: Caesar by means of generosity came to rule the empire, and many others, because they were generous and known to be so, eventually achieved greatness, I would answer: you are either a prince already or you are on the way to becoming one; in the first case, such generosity is harmful; in the second, it is certainly necessary to be thought of as generous. And Caesar was one of those who wished to become the ruler of Rome; but if, after having achieved this, he had lived and had not taken measures to moderate his spending, he would have destroyed that empire. And if someone were to reply: there have been many princes who with their troops have done great things, and have been considered very generous; I would answer: either a prince spends his own money and that of his subjects or he spends that of others; in the first case, he should be frugal; in the other, he should in no way hold back in his generosity. And to that prince who marches with his troops, who lives by plundering, sacking and ransom,

Ciro, Cesare e Alessandro; perchè lo spendere quello di altri non ti toglie reputazione, ma te ne aggiugne; solamente lo spendere il tuo è quello che ti nuoce. E non ci è cosa che consumi se stessa quanto la liberalità; la quale mentre che tu usi, perdi la facultà di usarla, e diventi o povero e contennendo, o, per fuggire la povertà, rapace e odioso. E intra tutte le cose di che uno principe si debbe guardare, è lo essere contennendo e odioso; e la liberalità all'una e l'altra cosa ti conduce. Pertanto è più sapienzia tenersi el nome del misero, che parturisce una infamia sanza odio, che, per volere el nome del liberale, essere necessitato incorrere nel nome del rapace, che parturisce una infamia con odio.

who controls what belongs to others, such generosity is essential; otherwise, his soldiers would not follow him. And with that which does not belong to you or to your subjects you can be a more liberal giver as was Cyrus, Caesar or Alexander, because spending what belongs to others does not detract from your reputation, rather it enhances it; only spending your own is what will hurt you. And there is nothing more self-consuming than generosity, for as you use it you are losing the means for using it, and you become either poor and despicable,[2] or, to escape poverty, rapacious and hated. And above all other things a prince must guard against being despicable and hated; and generosity leads you to both the one and the other. Consequently, it is wiser to put up with the name of miser, which gives birth to an infamy without hate, than to be obliged, because you wish to be known as generous, to incur the name of rapacious, which gives birth to an infamy with hate.

NOTES

1. The present King of France, Louis xii.

2. One becomes "despicable" as a result of being "poor," and "hated" as a result of being "rapacious."

XVII *De Crudelitate et Pietate; et an Sit Melius Amari Quam Timeri, Vel e Contra*

Scendendo appresso alle altre preallegate qualità, dico che ciascuno principe debbe desiderare di essere tenuto pietoso e non crudele; nondimanco debbe avvertire di non usare male questa pietà. Era tenuto Cesare Borgia crudele; nondimanco quella sua crudeltà aveva racconcia la Romagna, unitola, ridottola in pace e in fede. Il che se si considerrà bene, si vedrà quello essere stato molto più pietoso che il populo fiorentino; il quale, per fuggire el nome del crudele, lasciò distruggere Pistoia. Debbe, pertanto, uno principe non si curare della infamia di crudele, per tenere li sudditi sua uniti e in fede; perchè con pochissimi esempli, e' sarà più pietoso che quelli e quali, per troppa pietà, lasciono seguire e disordini, di che ne nasca occisioni o rapine; perchè queste sogliano offendere una universalità intera, e quelle esecuzioni che vengano dal principe offendano uno particulare. E intra tutti e principi, al principe nuovo è impossibile fuggire el nome del crudele, per essere li stati nuovi pieni di periculi. E Virgilio, nella bocca di Dido, dice:

> Res dura et regni novitas me talia cogunt
> Moliri, et late fines custode tueri.

Nondimanco debbe essere grave al credere e al muoversi, nè si fare paura da se stesso; e procedere in modo, temperato con prudenzia e umanità, che la troppa confidenzia non lo facci incauto e la troppa diffidenzia non lo renda intollerabile.

Nasce da questo una disputa: s'elli è meglio essere amato che temuto, o e converso. Respondesi che si vor-

person would like to be the one and the other; but since it is difficult to mix them together, it is much safer to be feared than loved, if one of the two must be lacking. For this can be generally said of men: they are ungrateful, fickle, liars and deceivers, avoiders of danger, greedy for profit; and as long as you serve their welfare, they are entirely yours, offering you their blood, possessions, life and children, as I mentioned earlier, when the occasion to do so is not in sight; but when you are faced with it, they turn against you. And that prince who lays his foundations on their promises alone, finding himself stripped of other preparations, falls to ruin; because friendships that are acquired with a price and not with excellence and nobility of character are bought, but they are not owned, and at the right time they cannot be spent. And men are less concerned with hurting someone who makes himself loved than one who makes himself feared, because love is held by a link of obligation, which, since men are wretched creatures, is broken every time their own interests are involved; but fear is held by a dread of punishment which will never leave you.

A prince must nevertheless make himself feared in such a way that if he does not gain love, he will avoid hate; because to be feared and not hated can go very well together; and this will always be the case so long as one abstains from the possessions of his citizens and subjects, and from their women. And should it become necessary for him to do away with someone, let him do it when there is convenient justification and manifest reason; but, above all, let him abstain from what belongs to others, for men forget more quickly the death of their fathers than the loss of their patrimony. Furthermore, reasons for taking another's possessions are never lacking, and inevitably he who begins to live by ravaging will find reasons for taking over what belongs to others; while, on

Ma quando el principe è con gli eserciti e ha in governo moltitudine di soldati, allora al tutto è necessario non si curare del nome del crudele; perchè, sanza questo nome, non si tenne mai esercito unito nè disposto ad alcuna fazione. Intra le mirabili azioni di Annibale si connumera questa; che, avendo uno esercito grossissimo, misto di infinite generazioni di uomini, condotto a militare in terre aliene, non vi surgessi mai alcuna dissensione, nè infra loro nè contro al principe, così nella cattiva come nella sua buona fortuna. Il che non potè nascere da altro che da quella sua inumana crudeltà, la quale, insieme con infinite sua virtù, lo fece sempre, nel conspetto de' suoi soldati, venerando e terrible; e sanza quella, a fare quello effetto, le altre sua virtù non li bastavano. E gli scrittori, in questo poco considerati, dall'una parte ammirano questa sua azione e dell'altra dannano la principale cagione di essa.

E che sia vero che l'altre sua virtù non sarebbano bastate, si può considerare in Scipione, rarissimo non solamente ne' tempi sua ma in tutta la memoria delle cose che si sanno; dal quale gli eserciti suoi in Ispagna si rebellorno; il che non nacque da altro che dalla troppa sua pietà, la quale aveva data a' suoi soldati più licenzia che alla disciplina militare non si conveniva. La qual cosa li fu da Fabio Massimo, in senato, rimproverata; e chiamato da lui corruttore della romana milizia. E Locrensi, sendo stati da uno legato di Scipione destrutti, non furono da lui vendicati, nè la insolenzia di quello legato corretta, nascendo tutto da quella sua natura facile; talmente che, volendolo alcuno in senato escusare, disse come egli erano di molti uomini che sapevano meglio non

the contrary, reasons for taking a life are more scarce, and they fade away more quickly.

But when the prince is with his troops and has command of many soldiers, then it is certainly imperative that he not care about the reputation of being cruel; because without such a reputation troops can never be kept united nor prepared for any combat. Among the admirable accomplishments of Hannibal[2] is numbered this: that, with a very large army, composed of men of all races, which he led into battle on foreign lands, there never arose any kind of dissension, neither among themselves nor against the prince, during his bad as well as good fortune. This could not have come about from anything other than that inhuman cruelty of his which, together with his many qualities, always made him revered and terrifying in the eyes of his men; and, without that, to achieve the same effect, his other qualities would not have been enough. And the writers, having reflected very little on this, on the one hand admire these accomplishments of his, and on the other they condemn the principal cause of them.

And that it is true that his other qualities would not have sufficed can be seen in the case of Scipio,[3] a most outstanding figure not only of his own time but of all recorded time, whose troops in Spain turned against him;[4] this came about from nothing other than his excessive leniency, which allowed his soldiers more liberty than the military code would normally provide. For this he was reproved in the Senate by Fabius Maximus,[5] who called him corruptor of the Roman army. The people of Locri, having been ruined by one of Scipio's officers, were not avenged by him, nor was the insolence of that officer checked, all this arising from his easy-going nature; so that, someone in the Senate wishing to free him of blame, said that there were many more men who knew

errare che correggere li errori. La quale natura arebbe col tempo violato la fama e la gloria di Scipione, se elli avessi con essa perseverato nello imperio; ma vivendo sotto el governo del senato, questa sua qualità dannosa non solum si nascose, ma li fu a gloria.

Concludo, adunque, tornando allo essere temuto e amato, che, amando li uomini a posta loro e temendo a posta del principe, debbe uno principe savio fondarsi in su quello che è suo, non in su quello che è d' altri; debbe solamente ingegnarsi di fuggire l' odio, come è detto.

how not to err better than they knew how to correct errors; such a nature in time would have damaged the fame and glory of Scipio, if he had maintained it during the empire; but living under the rule of the Senate, this harmful quality of his not only hid itself, but brought him glory.

I conclude, then, returning to the question of being feared and loved, that, since men love at their own pleasure, and fear at the pleasure of the prince, a wise prince should build his foundation on what is his own, not on what belongs to others: he must strive only to avoid hatred, as has been said.

NOTES

1. Verses from the *Aeneid*, ii, 563–64.

2. Hannibal (249–183 B.C.) was the chief commander of the Carthaginian armies who drove the war into Italy. He was conquered by Scipio at Zama in 202 B.C.

3. Scipio Africanus fought in Spain from 211 to 206. He then passed into Africa and conquered Hannibal, victoriously concluding the Second Punic War (218–202 B.C.).

4. In 206 A.D.

5. Consul of Rome and dictator in 217 B.C.

Quanto sia laudabile in uno principe mantenere la fede
e vivere con integrità e non con astuzia, ciascuno lo
intende; nondimanco si vede per esperienza ne' nostri
tempi quelli principi avere fatto gran cose, che della fede
hanno tenuto poco conto, e che hanno saputo con l'astuzia aggirare e cervelli delli uomini; e alla fine hanno su-
perato quelli che si sono fondati in su la lealtà.

Dovete, adunque, sapere come sono dua generazione di
combattere: l'uno, con le leggi; l'altro, con la forza; quel
primo è proprio dello uomo, quel secondo è delle bestie;
ma perchè il primo molte volte non basta, conviene ricorrere al secondo. Pertanto, a uno principe è necessario
sapere bene usare la bestia e l'uomo. Questa parte è suta
insegnata a' principi copertamente dalli antiqui scrittori;
li quali scrivono come Achille e molti altri di quelli
principi antichi furono dati a nutrire a Chirone centauro,
che sotto la sua disciplina li custodissi. Il che non vuole
dire altro, avere per precettore uno mezzo bestia e mezzo
uomo, se non che bisogna a uno principe sapere usare
l'una e l'altra natura; e l'una sanza l'altra non è durabile.
Sendo, dunque, uno principe necessitato sapere bene
usare la bestia, debbe di quelle pigliare la golpe e il lione;
perchè il lione non si defende da' lacci, la golpe non si
defende da' lupi. Bisogna, adunque, essere golpe a conoscere e lacci, e lione a sbigottire e lupi. Coloro che
stanno semplicemente in sul lione, non se ne intendano.
Non può, pertanto, uno signore prudente, nè debbe, osservare la fede, quando tale osservanzia li torni contro e che
sono spente le cagioni che la fecero promettere. E se gli
uomini fussino tutti buoni, questo precetto non sarebbe
buono; ma perchè sono tristi e non la osservarebbono a
te, tu etiam non l'hai ad osservare a loro. Nè mai a uno
principe mancorno cagioni legittime di colorire la inosser-

XVIII   *How a Prince Should Keep His Word*

How praiseworthy it is for a prince to keep his word and live by honesty and not deceit, everyone knows; nevertheless we see, by what goes on in our own times, that those princes who have accomplished great things are the ones who had cared little for keeping promises and who knew how to manipulate the minds of men with shrewdness; and in the end they won out over those who founded themselves on loyalty.

You should know, then, that there are two ways of fighting: one with the law, the other with force: the first way is peculiar to man, the other to beasts; but since the first in many instances is not enough, it becomes necessary to resort to the second. Therefore, a prince must know how to make good use of the beast and the man. This role was taught to princes indirectly by the ancient writers, who wrote how Achilles and many other ancient princes were given to Chiron the Centaur[1] to be brought up and trained under his direction. This can only mean, having as a teacher a half-beast and half-man, that a prince ought to know how to make use of both natures; and the one without the other cannot endure.

Since a prince must know how to make good use of the beast, he should choose then the fox and the lion; for the lion has no protection from traps, and the fox is defenseless against the wolves. It is necessary, therefore, to be a fox in order to know the traps, and a lion to frighten the wolves. Those who live by the lion alone do not understand matters. And so, a wise ruler cannot, nor should he, keep his word when doing so would be to his disadvantage and when the reasons that led him to make promises no longer exist. And if all men were good, this principle would not be good; but since men are a contemptible lot, and would not keep their promises to you, you too need not keep yours to them. To a prince legiti-

vanzia. Di questo se ne potrebbe dare infiniti esempli moderni, e mostrare quante paci, quante promesse sono state fatte irrite e vane per la infidelità de' principi; e quello che ha saputo meglio usare la golpe, è meglio capitato. Ma è necessario questa natura saperla bene colorire, ed essere gran simulatore e dissimulatore: e sono tanto semplici gli uomini, e tanto obediscano alle necessità presenti, che colui che inganna, troverrà sempre chi si lascerà ingannare.

Io non voglio, delli esempli freschi, tacerne uno. Alessandro vi non fece mai altro, non pensò mai ad altro che a ingannare uomini, e sempre trovò subietto da poterlo fare. E non fu mai uomo che avessi maggiore efficacia in asseverare, e con maggiori giuramenti affermassi una cosa, che la osservassi meno; nondimeno, sempre li succederono li inganni ad votum, perchè conosceva bene questa parte del mondo.

A uno principe, adunque, non è necessario avere in fatto tutte le soprascritte qualità, ma è bene necessario parere di averle. Anzi ardirò di dire questo: che, avendole e osservandole sempre, sono dannose; e parendo di averle, sono utili; come parere pietoso, fedele, umano, intero, religioso, ed essere; ma stare in modo edificato con l'animo, che, bisognando non essere, tu possa e sappi mutare el contrario. E hassi ad intendere questo: che uno principe, e massime uno principe nuovo, non può osservare tutte quelle cose per le quali gli uomini sono tenuti buoni, sendo spesso necessitato, per mantenere lo stato, operare contro alla fede, contro alla carità, contro alla umanità, contro alla religione. E però bisogna che egli abbi uno animo disposto a volgersi secondo ch'e venti della fortuna e le variazioni delle cose li comandano, e, come di sopra dissi, non partirsi dal bene, potendo, ma sapere intrare nel male, necessitato.

mate reasons to break promises are never lacking. Of this an infinite number of present-day examples could be noted, indicating how many peace treaties, how many promises have been made null and void by the unfaithfulness of princes: and he who has known best how to use the fox has come to a better end. But one must know how to disguise this nature well, and how to be a fine liar and hypocrite; and men are so simple-minded and so dominated by their present needs that one who deceives will always find one who will allow himself to be deceived.

There is one of these recent examples I do not wish to be silent about. Alexander vi did nothing else, he thought about nothing else, except to deceive men, and he always found the occasion to do it. And never was there a man more forceful in his assertions, and who affirmed a thing with more promises who kept his word less; nevertheless, the deceits he planned were always successful, because he was well acquainted with this facet of life.

It is not necessary, then, for a prince to have all of the qualities mentioned above, but it is certainly necessary that he appear to have them. In fact, I would go so far as to say this, that having them and observing them at all times, they are harmful; and appearing to have them, they are useful; for example, appearing to be compassionate, faithful, humane, upright, religious, and being so; but his mind should be disposed in such a way that should it become necessary not to be so, he will be able and know how to change to the contrary. And it must be understood that a prince, and in particular a new prince, cannot observe all those things by which men are considered good, for it is often necessary, in order to maintain the state, to act against your word, against charity, against kindness, against religion. And so, he must have a mind ready to turn itself according as the winds of fortune and the fluctuation of things command him, and, as I said

Debbe, adunque, avere uno principe gran cura che non li esca mai di bocca una cosa che non sia piena delle soprascritte cinque qualità; e paia, a vederlo e udirlo, tutto pietà, tutto fede, tutto integrità, tutto umanità, tutto religione. E non è cosa più necessaria a parere di avere che questa ultima qualità. E li uomini, in universali, iudicano più alli occhi che alle mani; perchè tocca a vedere a ognuno, a sentire a pochi. Ognuno vede quello che tu pari, pochi sentono quello che tu se'; e quelli pochi non ardiscano opporsi alla opinione di molti che abbino la maestà dello stato che gli defenda; e nelle azioni di tutti gli uomini, e massime de' principi, dove non è iudizio a chi reclamare, si guarda al fine. Facci dunque uno principe di vincere e mantenere lo stato; e mezzi saranno sempre iudicati onorevoli e da ciascuno laudati; perchè il vulgo ne va sempre preso con quello che pare e con lo evento della cosa; e nel mondo non è se non vulgo; e li pochi non ci hanno luogo quando li assai hanno dove appoggiarsi. Alcuno principe de' presenti tempi, quale non è bene nominare, non predica mai altro che pace e fede, e dell' una e dell' altra è inimicissimo; e l' una e l' altra, quando e' l' avessi osservata, gli arebbe più volte tolto o la reputazione o lo stato.

above, he must not separate himself from the good, if he is able, but he must know how to take up evil, should it become necessary.

A prince, therefore, should take great care never to say a single thing that is not infused with the five qualities mentioned above; he should appear, when seen and heard, to be all compassion, all faithfulness, all integrity, all kindness, all religion. And nothing is more essential than to appear to have this last quality. And men, in general, judge more according to their eyes than their hands; since everyone is in a position to observe, just a few to touch. Everyone sees what you appear to be, few touch what you are; and those few do not dare oppose the opinions of the many who have the majesty of the state defending them; and with regard to the actions of all men, and especially with princes where there is no court of appeal, we must look at the final result. Let a prince, then, conquer and maintain the state; his methods will always be judged honorable and they will be praised by all; because the ordinary people are always taken by the appearance and the outcome of a thing; and in the world there is nothing but ordinary people; and there is no room for the few while the many have a place to lean on. A certain prince[2] in our own time, whose name is better left unmentioned, preaches nothing but peace and good faith, and he is exceedingly hostile to both of them; and if he had put both of them into practice on more than one occasion they would have lost him either his reputation or his state.

NOTES

1. A Greek mythological figure, half horse and half man, he was the son of Saturn and the nymph Philyra.

2. Ferdinand the Catholic.

Ma perchè, circa le qualità di che di sopra si fa menzione, io ho parlato delle più importanti, l'altre voglio discorrere brevemente sotto queste generalità: che il principe pensi, come di sopra in parte è detto, di fuggire quelle cose che lo faccino odioso o contennendo; e qualunque volta fuggirà questo, arà adempiuto le parti sua e non troverrà nelle altre infamie periculo alcuno. Odioso lo fa, sopra tutto, come io dissi, lo essere rapace e usurpatore della roba e delle donne de' sudditi; di che si debbe astenere; e qualunque volta alle universalità delli uomini non si toglie nè roba nè onore, vivono contenti; e solo si ha a combattere con la ambizione di pochi, la quale in molti modi e con facilità si raffrena. Contennendo lo fa essere tenuto vario, leggieri, effeminato, pusillanime, irresoluto; da che uno principe si debbe guardare come da uno scoglio, e ingegnarsi che nelle azioni sua si riconosca grandezza, animosità, gravità, fortezza; e circa e maneggi privati de' sudditi, volere che la sua sentenzia sia inrevocabile; e si mantenga in tale opinione che alcuno non pensi nè a ingannarlo nè ad aggirarlo.

Quel principe che dà di sè questa opinione, è reputato assai; e contro a chi è reputato con difficultà si coniura, con difficultà è assaltato, purchè si intenda che sia eccellente e reverito da' suoi. Perchè uno principe debbe avere dua paure: una drento, per conto de' sudditi; l'altra di fuora, per conto de' potentati esterni. Da questa si difende con le buone arme e con li buoni amici; e sempre, se arà buone arme, arà buoni amici; e sempre staranno ferme le cose di drento, quando stieno ferme quelle di fuora, se già le non fussero perturbate da una coniura; e quando pure quelle di fuora movessino, s'egli è ordi-

XIX   On Avoiding Being Disdained and Hated

But now that I have talked about the most important of the qualities mentioned above, I would like to discuss the others briefly in this general way: that a prince, as was mentioned in part above,[1] should concentrate on avoiding those things that may render him hateful and contemptible; and when he has avoided this, he will have fulfilled his duties and will find no danger in his other vices. What makes him hated above all, as I have said,[2] is being rapacious and a usurper of the property and the women belonging to his subjects: he must abstain from this; for the majority of men, so long as you do not deprive them of their possessions and honor, live happily; and you have only to contend with the ambition of a few who can be kept in check easily and in many ways. He is contemptible if he is thought of as changeable, frivolous, effeminate, cowardly, irresolute: a prince should be on his guard for these things as he would for a reef, and he should strive in such a way that in his actions will be recognized magnanimity, courageousness, seriousness, and strength; and in regard to the private affairs of his subjects, he should insist that his judgment be irrevocable; and he should be regarded in such a way that no one would think of deceiving him or cheating him.

That prince who gives such an impression of himself is highly esteemed; and it is difficult to conspire against one who is esteemed, and difficult to attack him, provided that it is understood he is an outstanding man and respected by his subjects. For a prince must have two fears: one internal, in regard to his subjects; the other external, in regard to outside powers. From the latter he can defend himself with good armed forces and good friends; and if he has good armed forces he will always have good friends; and internal affairs will always remain stabilized when those outside are stable, on condition that they

nato e vissuto come ho detto, quando non si abbandoni, sempre sosterrà ogni impeto, come io dissi che fece Nabide spartano. Ma circa a'sudditi, quando le cose di fuora non muovino, si ha a temere che non coniurino secretamente: del che il principe si assicura assai, fuggendo lo essere odiato o disprezzato, e tenendosi le populo satisfatto di lui; il che è necessario conseguire, come di sopra a lungo si disse. E uno de' più potenti rimedii che abbi uno principe contro alle coniure, è non essere odiato dallo universale; perchè sempre chi coniura crede, con la morte del principe, satisfare al populo; ma quando e' creda offenderlo, non piglia animo a prendere simile partito; perchè le difficultà che sono dalla parte de' coniuranti sono infinite. E per esperienza si vede molte essere state le coniure e poche avere avuto buon fine; perchè chi coniura non può essere solo, nè può prendere compagnia se non di quelli che creda esser mal contenti; e subito che a uno mal contento tu hai scoperto l'animo tuo, li dài materia a contentarsi, perchè manifestamente lui ne può sperare ogni commodità; talmente che, veggendo el guadagno fermo da questa parte, e dall'altra veggendolo dubbio e pieno di periculo, conviene bene o che sia raro amico, o che sia al tutto ostinato inimico del principe, ad osservarti la fede. E per ridurre la cosa in brevi termini, dico che dalla parte del coniurante non è se non paura, gelosia, sospetto di pena che lo sbigottisce; ma dalla parte del principe è la maestà del principato, le leggi, le difese delli amici e dello stato che lo difendano; talmente che, aggiunto a tutte queste cose la benivolenzia populare, è impossibile che alcuno sia sì temerario che coniuri. Perchè, per lo ordinario, dove uno coniurante ha a temere innanzi alla esecuzione del male, in questo caso debbe temere ancora poi (avendo per inimico el popolo) seguìto lo eccesso, nè potendo per questo sperare refugio alcuno.

have not already been disturbed by conspiracy; and even
when outside conditions shift, if he is organized and has
lived the way I have prescribed, if he does not lose control of himself, he will always be able to withstand every
blow, just as I said the Spartan Nabis did. But in regard
to his subjects, when outside affairs are not shifting, there
may be fear of secret conspiracy, from which the prince
best protects himself by avoiding being hated or disdained, and by maintaining the people's satisfaction with
him—which is a necessary accomplishment, as was discussed above at length.[3] And one of the most powerful
remedies a prince has against conspiracies is not to be
hated by the majority: for the one who conspires always
thinks that by killing the prince he will satisfy the people;
but when he thinks he might offend them, he has no
courage to undertake such an enterprise, for the difficulties on the side of the conspirators are infinite. And
experience shows that the number of conspiracies are
many, but few have come to a good end; for he who
conspires cannot be on his own nor can he choose com-
panions from any if not from those whom he believes
to be malcontent; and as soon as you have revealed yourself to one malcontent, you provide him with the means
to become content, for in revealing this plan he can
hope to have everything he wants: to the extent that,
seeing that the gain is certain on the one side, while on
the other it is uncertain and full of dangers, he would
either have to be an unusual kind of friend indeed, or a
truly sworn enemy of the prince, in order to keep faith
with you. To put it briefly, let me say that on the side
of the conspirator there is nothing but fear, jealousy
and the prospect of punishment that haunts him; but
on the side of the prince, there is the majesty of the
principality, the laws, the protection of friends and the
government to defend him: so that, with the good will

Di questa materia se ne potria dare infiniti esempli;
ma voglio solo essere contento di uno, seguìto alla memoria de' padri nostri. Messer Annibale Bentivogli, avolo
del presente messer Annibale, che era principe in Bologna,
sendo da' Canneschi, che gli coniurorono contro, ammazzato, nè rimanendo di lui altri che messer Giovanni, che
era in fasce, subito dopo tale omicidio, si levò il populo
e ammazzò tutti e Canneschi. Il che nacque dalla benivolenzia populare che la casa de' Bentivogli aveva in quelli
tempi; la quale fu tanta che, non restando di quella alcuno in Bologna che potessi, morto Annibale, reggere lo
stato, e avendo indizio come in Firenze era uno nato de'
Bentivogli che si teneva fino allora figliuolo di un fabbro,
vennero e Bolognesi per quello in Firenze, e li dettero el
governo di quella città; la quale fu governata da lui fino
a tanto che messer Giovanni pervenissi in età conveniente
al governo.

Concludo, pertanto, che uno principe debbe tenere
delle coniure poco conto, quando el popolo gli sia benivolo; ma, quando li sia nimico e abbilo in odio, debbe
temere d'ogni cosa e d'ognuno. E li stati bene ordinati
e li principi savii hanno con ogni diligenzia pensato di
non desperare e grandi e di satisfare al populo e tenerlo
contento; perchè questa è una delle più importanti ma-
terie che abbi uno principe.

of the people added to all these things, it is impossible for someone to be so rash as to conspire against him. For, where ordinarily a conspirator has to fear before he performs his evil, in this instance he has also to fear after the crime has been committed (when he has the people as his enemy), nor can he, because of this, hope to find any refuge whatsoever.

Endless examples dealing with this matter could be cited; but I shall be satisfied to give one that took place during the time of our fathers. When Messer Annibale Bentivogli, prince of Bologna and grandfather of the present Messer Annibale, was murdered by the Canneschi, who had conspired against him, he left behind him no one except Messer Giovanni, who was a babe in arms. Immediately after this homicide, the people rose up and killed all the Canneschi. This resulted from the good will of the people which the house of Bentivogli had at that time: so much good will that, with Annibale dead and there being no remaining survivor of that house in Bologna who could rule the state, the Bolognese people, having heard that there was someone in Florence of Bentivogli blood who until that time was believed to be the son of a blacksmith, went to Florence to get him, and they gave him the government of their city: it was governed by him until Messer Giovanni became of age to rule.[4]

I conclude, then, that a prince should not be too concerned with conspiracies, when he has the good will of the people; but when they are hostile toward him and bear him hatred, he should fear everything and everybody. And well-organized states and wise princes have in every way taken care not to infuriate the nobles, and to satisfy the common people and keep them happy; for this is one of the most important functions a prince has.

Intra e regni bene ordinati e governati a' tempi nostri è quello di Francia; e in esso si truovano infinite costituzione buone, donde depende la libertà e securtà del re; delle quali la prima è il parlamento e la sua autorità. Perchè quello che ordinò quel regno, conoscendo la ambizione de' potenti e la insolenzia loro, e iudicando essere loro necessario uno freno in bocca che li correggessi, e dall'altra parte conoscendo l'odio dello universale contro a' grandi fondato in su la paura, e volendo assicurarli, non volse che questa fussi particulare cura del re, per torli quel carico ch'e' potessi avere co' grandi favorendo e populari, e con li populari favorendo e grandi; e però costituì uno iudice terzo, che fussi quello che, sanza carico del re, battessi e grandi e favorissi e minori. Nè possè essere questo ordine migliore nè più prudente, nè che sia maggiore cagione della securtà del re e del regno. Di che si può trarre un altro notabile: che li principi debbano le cose di carico fare sumministrare ad altri, quelle di grazia a loro medesimi. Di nuovo concludo che uno principe debbe stimare e grandi, ma non si fare odiare dal populo.

Parrebbe forse a molti, considerato la vita e morte di alcuno imperatore romano, che fussino esempli contrarii a questa mia opinione; trovando alcuno essere vissuto sempre egregiamente e mostro grande virtù d'animo, nondimeno avere perso l'imperio, o vero essere stato morto da' sua che gli hanno coniurato contro. Volendo, pertanto, rispondere a queste obiezioni, discorrerò le qualità di alcuni imperatori, mostrando le cagioni della loro ruina, non disforme da quello che da me si è addutto; e parte metterò in considerazione quelle cose che sono notabili a chi legge le azioni di quelli tempi. E voglio mi basti

Among those kingdoms in our times that are organized and governed well is that of France: in it are found numerous good institutions upon which the freedom and safety of the king depend. Of these the first is the parliament and its authority; for he who organized that kingdom, being aware of the ambitions and arrogance of the nobles and realizing the necessity of keeping a bit in their mouths in order to restrain them, while, on the other hand, being aware of the hatred, based on fear, of the masses for the nobles, and wishing to reassure them, did not want this to be a particular obligation of the king; so that he would be relieved of that pressure which he might incur from the nobles in favoring the common people and from the common people in favoring the nobles, he established a third arbiter[5] that might, without burdening the king, repress the nobles and favor the lower classes. There could not be a better or wiser system, nor could there be a better measure of security for the king and the kingdom. From this another noteworthy point can be drawn: that princes should delegate unpleasant obligations to others;[6] those pleasant ones he should keep for himself. Again let me conclude by saying that a prince should respect the nobles, but not make himself hated by the people.

Perhaps it may seem to many who have studied the lives and deaths of a number of Roman emperors that they afford examples contrary to my viewpoint just expressed, for we shall discover that some of them have lived consistently noble lives and displayed great strength of character but have, nonetheless, lost their empire, or, indeed, have been killed by their own people who conspired against them. And so, wishing to answer these objections, I shall discuss the characters of several of these emperors, pointing out the reasons for their downfall which are not unlike those that I myself have deduced;

pigliare tutti quelli imperatori che succederono allo imperio da Marco filosofo a Massimino: e quali furono, Marco, Commodo suo figliuolo, Pertinace, Iuliano, Severo, Antonino Caracalla suo figliuolo, Macrino, Eliogabalo, Alessandro e Massimino. Ed è prima da notare che, dove nelli altri principati si ha solo a contendere con la ambizione de' grandi e insolenzia de' populi, li imperatori romani avevano una terza difficultà: di avere a sopportare la crudeltà e averizia de' soldati. La qual cosa era sì difficile che la fu cagione della ruina di molti, sendo difficile satisfare a' soldati e a' populi; perchè e populi amavano la quiete, e per questo amavano e principi modesti, e li soldati amavano el principe che fussi di animo militare e che fussi insolente, crudele e rapace; le quali cose volevono che lui esercitassi ne' populi, per potere avere duplicato stipendio e sfogare la loro avarizia e crudeltà. Le quali cose feciono che quelli imperatori che, per natura o per arte, non avevano una grande reputazione, tale che con quella tenessino l'uno e l'altro in freno, sempre ruinavono; e li più di loro, massime quelli che come uomini nuovi venivano al principato, conosciuta la difficultà di questi dua diversi umori, si volgevano a satisfare a' soldati, stimando poco lo iniuriare el populo. Il quale partito era necessario; perchè, non potendo e principi mancare di non essere odiati da qualcuno, si debbano prima forzare di non essere odiati dalla università; e quando non possano conseguire questo, si debbano ingegnare con ogni industria fuggire l'odio di quelle università che sono più potenti. E però quelli imperatori che, per novità, avevano bisogno di favori estraordinarii, si aderivano a' soldati più tosto che a' populi; il che tornava loro, nondimeno, utile o no, secondo che quel principe si sapeva mantenere reputato con loro.

and at the same time I shall submit for consideration
those things that are worth noticing to whoever reads the
history of those times. And I shall let it suffice to take
all those emperors who came to reign from Marcus the
philosopher to Maximinus:[7] these were Marcus, his son
Commodus, Pertinax, Julian, Severus, his son Antonio
Caracalla, Macrinus, Heliogabalus, Alexander and Maximinus. And first, it is to be noted that while in other
principalities there is only the ambition of the nobles and
the insubordination of the people to contend with, the
Roman Emperors had a third difficulty: having to put up
with the cruelty and greediness of their soldiers. This was
such a difficult thing that it became the cause of the
downfall of many, because it was difficult to satisfy the
soldiers and the people; for the people loved tranquility,
and for this reason they loved peaceful princes, and the
soldiers loved a prince who had a military flair and who
was aggresive, cruel and rapacious; they wanted him to
practice such traits on the people so that they might
double their wages and give vent to their greediness and
cruelty. Whereby those emperors who through natural
ability or political strategy had not acquired great reputation, such that would enable them to hold both the
people and the soldiers in harness, always came to ruin.
And the majority of them, especially those who were new
to the government, having recognized the difficulty arising from these two diverse dispositions, turned to satisfying the soldiers, caring little of offending the people. Such
a policy was necessary: since princes cannot help being
hated by somebody, they must above all endeavor not
to be hated by a group of people; and when they are
unable to achieve this, they should strive in every way to
avoid the hatred of the most powerful group. And so
those emperors, who because they were new needed a
great deal of backing, sided with the soldiers rather than

Da queste cagioni sopradette nacque che Marco, Pertinace e Alessandro, sendo tutti di modesta vita, amatori della iustizia, inimici della crudeltà, umani, benigni, ebbono tutti, da Marco in fuora, tristo fine. Marco solo visse e morì onoratissimo, perchè lui succedè allo imperio iure hereditario, e non aveva a riconoscere quello nè da' soldati nè da' populi; di poi, sendo accompagnato da molte virtù che lo facevano venerando, tenne sempre, mentre che visse, l'uno ordine e l'altro intra e termini sua, e non fu mai nè odiato nè disprezzato. Ma Pertinace, creato imperatore contro alla voglia de' soldati, li quali, sendo usi a vivere licenziosamente sotto Commodo, non poterono sopportare quella vita onesta alla quale Pertinace gli voleva ridurre, onde avendosi creato odio, e a questo odio aggiunto el disprezzo sendo vecchio, ruinò ne' primi principii della sua amministrazione.

E qui si debbe notare che l'odio s'acquista così mediante le buone opere, come le triste; e però, come io dissi di sopra, volendo uno principe mantenere lo stato, è spesso forzato a non essere buono; perchè, quando quella università, o populo o soldati o grandi che sieno, della quale tu iudichi, per mantenerti, avere bisogno, è corrotta, ti conviene seguire l'umore suo per satisfarle; e allora le buone opere ti sono nimiche. Ma vegnamo ad Alessandro; il quale fu di tanta bontà che, intra le altre laude che li sono attribuite, è questa: che in quattordici anni che tenne lo imperio, non fu mai morto da lui alcuno iniudicato; nondimanco, sendo tenuto effeminato e uomo che si lasciassi governare alla madre, e per questo venuto in disprezzo, conspirò in lui lo esercito, e ammazzollo.

with the people; nevertheless, this turned out to be for them either useful or not, according to whether that prince knew how to maintain his standing with them.

For the reasons mentioned above it happened that Marcus, Pertinax and Alexander, all of whom led restrained lives, were lovers of justice, enemies of cruelty, genial and kind, all, except for Marcus, came to a sad end. Marcus[8] alone lived and died with great esteem, because he had succeeded to the empire with hereditary rights and did not have to be grateful for it either to the soldiers or the people; then, endowed with many qualities that made him respected, he always held, while he was alive, both the one faction and the other within their bounds, and he was never hated or disdained. But Pertinax[9] was made Emperor against the will of the soldiers, who, since they were accustomed to licentious living under Commodus, could not put up with that decent way of life to which Pertinax wished to reduce them, whereby having brought upon himself this hatred to which was added contempt, for he was old, he came to ruin at the very beginning of his administration.

And here it should be noted that hate may be acquired by way of good deeds as by bad ones: and so, as I said above, if a prince wishes to hold on to the state, he is often forced into not being good; for, whenever that group which you think you need to sustain you is corrupt, whether it be the people or the soldiers or the nobles, it is to your advantage to adopt their disposition in order to satisfy them; and then good deeds are your enemies. But let us come to Alexander:[10] he was of such goodness that among the other praiseworthy things ascribed to him there is this one, that during the fourteen years that he held the empire no one was put to death by him without a trial; however, since he was considered effeminate, and a man who allowed himself to be governed by his mother,

Discorrendo ora, per opposito, le qualità di Commodo, di Severo, Antonino Caracalla e Massimino, li troverrete crudelissimi e rapaccissimi; li quali, per satisfare a' soldati, non perdonorono ad alcuna qualità di iniuria che ne' populi si potessi commettere; e tutti, eccetto Severo, ebbono triste fine. Perchè in Severo fu tanta virtù che, mantenendosi e soldati amici, ancora che i populi fussino da lui gravati, possè sempre regnare felicemente; perchè quelle sua virtù lo facevano nel conspetto de' soldati e de' populi sì mirabile, che questi rimanevano quodam modo attoniti e stupidi, e quelli altri reverenti e satisfatti.

E perchè le azioni di costui furono grandi e notabile in uno principe nuovo, io voglio mostrare brevemente quanto bene seppe usare la persona della golpe e del lione; le quali nature io dico di sopra essere necessarie imitare a uno principe. Conosciuto Severo la ignavia di Iuliano imperatore, persuase al suo esercito, del quale era in Stiavonia capitano, che gli era bene andare a Roma a vendicare la morte di Pertinace, el quale da' soldati pretoriani era suto morto. E sotto questo colore, sanza mostrare di aspirare allo imperio, mosse lo esercito contro a Roma, e fu prima in Italia che si sapessi la sua partita. Arrivato a Roma, fu dal senato, per timore, eletto imperatore e morto Iuliano. Restava, dopo questo principio, a Severo due difficultà, volendosi insignorire di tutto lo stato: l'una, in Asia dove Pescennio Nigro, capo delli eserciti asiatici, si era fatto chiamare imperatore; e l'altra in ponente, dove era Albino, quale ancora lui aspirava allo imperio. E perchè iudicava periculoso scoprirsi inimico a tutti a dua, deliberò di assaltare Nigro e ingannare Albino. Al quale scrisse come, sendo dal senato eletto imperatore, voleva partecipare quella dignità con lui; e

for this reason he came to be disdained, and the army conspired against him and murdered him.

Discussing now, in contrast, the characters of Commodus, Severus, Antonius Caracalla and Maximinus, you will find them very cruel and extremely rapacious; in order to satisfy the soldiers they did not abstain from inflicting all kinds of injury on the people; and all of them, except Severus,[11] came to a sad end. Because Severus possessed such ingenuity that, maintaining the soldiers as friends even though the people were oppressed by him, he was always able to reign successfully; for those qualities of his made him, in the eyes of the soldiers and the people, so admirable that the former were astonished and stunned and the others respectful and satisfied.

And since his actions were so outstanding and noteworthy for a new prince, I wish to show briefly how well he knew how to employ the nature of the fox and the lion: it is necessary, as I say above,[12] for a prince to imitate such natures. When Severus learned of the indolence of the emperor Julianus, he persuaded his troops, of which he was in command in Slavonia, that it would be a good thing to go to Rome to vindicate the death of Pertinax, who had been murdered by the Pretorian guards. And under this pretext, without seeming to aspire to the empire, he led the army against Rome; and he was in Italy before his departure was known. After his arrival in Rome, the senate, out of fear, elected him emperor and killed Julianus. There remained, after this beginning, two difficulties for Severus if he wished to become master of the entire state: one in Asia, where Pescennius Niger, commander of the Asiatic army, had himself proclaimed emperor; and the other in the west where there was Albinus, who also aspired to the empire. And since he thought it dangerous to show himself hostile to both of them, he decided to attack Niger and deceive Albinus.

mandolli el titulo di Cesare e, per deliberazione del senato, se lo aggiunse collega; le quali cose furono da Albino accettate per vere. Ma poi che Severo ebbe vinto e morto Nigro, e pacate le cose orientali, ritornatosi a Roma, si querelò, in senato, come Albino, poco conoscente de' benefizii ricevuti da lui, aveva dolosamente cerco di ammazzarlo; e per questo lui era necessitato andare a punire la sua ingratitudine. Di poi andò a trovarlo in Francia, e li tolse lo stato e la vita.

Chi esaminerà, adunque, tritamente le azioni di costui, lo troverrà uno ferocissimo lione e una astutissima golpe; e vedrà quello temuto e reverito da ciascuno, e dalli eserciti non odiato; e non si maraviglierà se lui, uomo nuovo, arà possuto tenere tanto imperio; perchè la sua grandissima reputazione lo difese sempre da quello odio che e populi per le sue rapine avevano potuto concipere. Ma Antonino, suo figliuolo, fu ancora lui uomo che aveva parte eccellentissime e che lo facevano maraviglioso nel conspetto de' populi e grato a' soldati; perchè era uomo militare, sopportantissimo d' ogni fatica, disprezzatore d' ogni cibo delicato e d' ogni altra mollizia; la qual cosa lo faceva amare da tutti li eserciti; nondimanco la sua ferocia e crudeltà fu tanta e sì inaudita, per avere, dopo infinite occisioni particulari, morto gran parte del populo di Roma e tutto quello di Alessandria, che diventò odiosissimo a tutto il mondo, e cominciò ad essere temuto etiam da quelli che lui aveva intorno; in modo che fu ammazzato da uno centurione, in mezzo del suo esercito. Dove è da notare che queste simili morti, le quali seguano per deliberazione di uno animo ostinato, sono da' principi inevitabili, perchè ciascuno che non si curi di morire lo può offendere; ma debbe bene el principe temerne meno,

He wrote to the latter saying that, having been elected
emperor by the senate, he wanted to share that dignity
with him; and he sent him the title of Cesar and, with
the consent of the senate, took him as his co-leader:
these things were accepted by Albinus as the truth. But
after Severus had conquered and killed Niger and pacified
things in the east, returning to Rome, he complained to
the senate that Albinus, not very grateful for the favors
received from him, had treacherously sought to murder
him, and for this reason it would be necessary for him
to go and punish his ingratitude. Then he went to seek
him out in France, and took both his state and his life.

Whoever, therefore, examines carefully the actions of
this man will find him a very fierce lion and a most cunning fox; he will see that he was feared and respected by
everyone and not hated by the troops; and he will not be
surprised if he, a new man, was able to maintain so great
an empire; for his enormous reputation always protected
him from that hatred that the people could have conceived
against him because of his plundering. Now Antonius,[13] his
son, was also a man who had excellent points that made
him admirable in the eyes of the people and pleasing to
the soldiers; for he was a military man, very able to put
up with all kinds of exertion, disdainful of any fancy food
and of every other kind of luxurious living: this made
him loved by all the troops; nevertheless his ferocity and
cruelty was so great and so unheard of—having, after innumerable individual slayings, put to death a large part
of the Roman populace and all of Alexandria's—that he
became exceedingly hateful to all the world. And he
began to be feared also by those he had around him; so
that he was murdered by a centurion in the midst of
his army. Wherefore it should be noted that deaths such
as these, that result from the deliberation of a determined
individual, are unavoidable for princes; for anyone who

perchè le sono rarissime. Debbe solo guardarsi di non fare grave iniuria ad alcuno di coloro de' quali si serve e che gli ha d'intorno al servizio del suo principato: come aveva fatto Antonino, il quale aveva morto contumeliosamente uno fratello di quel centurione, e lui ogni giorno minacciava; tamen lo teneva a guardia del corpo suo; il che era partito temerario e da ruinarvi come li intervenne.

Ma vegnamo a Commodo; al quale era facilità grande tenere lo imperio, per averlo iure hereditario, sendo figliuolo di Marco; e solo li bastava seguire le vestigie del padre, e a' soldati e a' populi arebbe satisfatto. Ma sendo d'animo crudele e bestiale, per potere usare la sua rapacità ne' populi, si volse a intrattenere li eserciti e farli licenziosi; dall'altra parte, non tenendo la sua dignità, discendendo spesso ne' teatri a combattere co' gladiatori e faccendo altre cose vilissime e poco degne della maestà imperiale, diventò contennendo nel conspetto de' soldati. Ed essendo odiato dall'una parte e disprezzato dall'altra, fu conspirato in lui, e morto.

Restaci a narrare le qualità di Massimino. Costui fu uomo bellicosissimo; ed essendo li eserciti infastiditi della mollizie di Alessandro, del quale ho di sopra discorso, morto lui, lo elessono allo imperio. Il quale non molto tempo possedè, perchè dua cose lo feciono odioso e contennendo: l'una, essere vilissimo per avere già guardato le pecore in Tracia (la qual cosa era per tutto notissima e li faceva una grande dedignazione nel conspetto di qualunque); l'altra, perchè, avendo nello ingresso del suo principato differito lo andare a Roma ed entrare nella pos-

is not concerned about dying can do him harm; but the prince need not be too afraid of them, for they are very rare. He need only be on the alert not to inflict serious injury on anyone who serves him or whom he has around him in the service of the principality: just as Antonius had done when he shamefully put to death the brother of that centurion; and he would threaten him every day despite the fact that he kept him as a bodyguard—this was a rash undertaking and, as it happened, brought about his downfall.

But let us come to Commodus,[14] for whom it was very easy to hold on to the empire, since he acquired it through hereditary right, being the son of Marcus; and it would have been enough merely for him to follow in the footsteps of his father to satisfy the soldiers and the people. But being a cruel and brutal individual, in order to practice his rapacity on the people he turned to indulging the armies and made them licentious; on the other hand, in not maintaining his dignity by frequently descending into the arena to fight with the gladiators and by doing other very vile things hardly worthy of the imperial majesty, he became contemptible in the eyes of the soldiers. And being hated on the one side and disdained on the other, he was conspired against and killed.

There remains to tell of the qualities of Maximinus.[15] He was a very warlike person, and since the armies were annoyed with the effeminacy of Alexander, which I discussed above, they elected him to the empire after Alexander's death. He was not in possession of it very long, for two things made him hateful and disdained: one, his base origin, having at one time herded sheep in Thrace (this fact was well known everywhere and caused him to be greatly disdained in the eyes of everyone); the other, because, at the beginning of his reign having deferred

sessione della sedia imperiale, aveva dato di sè opinione di crudelissimo, avendo per li sua prefetti, in Roma e in qualunque luogo dello imperio, esercitato molte crudeltà. Tal che, commosso tutto el mondo dallo sdegno per la viltà del suo sangue e dallo odio per la paura della sua ferocia, si rebellò prima Affrica, di poi el senato con tutto el popolo di Roma; e tutta Italia li conspirò contro. A che si aggiunse el suo proprio esercito; quale, campeggiando Aquileia e trovando difficultà nella espugnazione, infastidito della crudeltà sua, e per vederli tanti inimici temendolo meno, lo ammazzò.

Io non voglio ragionare nè di Eliogabalo nè di Macrino nè di Iuliano, e quali, per essere al tutto contennendi, si spensero subito; ma verrò alla conclusione di questo discorso. E dico che gli principi de' nostri tempi hanno meno questa difficultà di satisfare estraordinariamente a' soldati ne' governi loro; perchè, nonostante che si abbi ad avere a quelli qualche considerazione, tamen si resolve presto, per non avere, alcuno di questi principi, eserciti insieme che sieno inveterati con li governi e amministrazione delle provincie, come erano li eserciti dello imperio romano. E però, se allora era necessario satisfare più a' soldati che a' populi, era perch' e soldati potevano più che e populi; ora è più necessario a tutti e principi, eccetto che al Turco e al Soldano, satisfare a' populi che a' soldati, perchè e populi possono più di quelli. Di che io ne eccettuo el Turco, tenendo sempre quello intorno a sè dodicimila fanti e quindicimila cavalli, da' quali depende la securtà e la fortezza del suo regno; ed è necessario che, posposto ogni altro respetto, quel signore se li mantenga amici. Similmente el regno del Soldano sendo tutto in mano de' soldati, conviene che ancora lui, sanza respetto de' populi, se li mantenga amici. E avete a notare

his trip to Rome to take possession of the imperial throne, he gave the impression of being extremely cruel, having through his prefects, in Rome and in all parts of the empire, exercised numerous cruelties. So that, with the entire world moved by disdain for the baseness of his origin and the hatred caused by fear of his ferocity, Africa rebelled first, then the senate with all the people of Rome; and all of Italy conspired against him. His own army joined with them, for, while besieging Aquileia and finding the battle difficult, disgusted with his cruelty, and seeing that he had so many enemies, they feared him less and killed him.

I shall not discuss Heliogabalus[16] nor Macrinus[17] nor Julianus[18] who, because they were thoroughly contemptible, were soon done away with; rather, I shall come to the conclusion of this discourse by saying that the princes of our time have less of this difficulty of satisfying the soldiers in their states by inordinate means; for, though certain considerations should be shown toward them, any difficulties are quickly resolved, for none of these princes have standing armies that are connected with the government and the administration of the provinces as were the armies of the Roman Empire. And so, if at one time it was necessary to satisfy the soldiers more than the people, it was because the soldiers could do more than the people; now it is more necessary for all princes, except the Turk and the Sultan, to satisfy the people rather than the soldiers, because the people can do more than the soldiers. I make an exception of the Turk, because he always keeps around him twelve thousand foot soldiers and fifteen thousand horsemen, on whom depend the security and the strength of his realm, and it is necessary that all other considerations be secondary to that ruler's maintaining their friendship. Similarly with the realm of the

che questo stato del Soldano è disforme da tutti li altri principati, perchè elli è simile al pontificato cristiano; il quale non si può chiamare nè principato ereditario, nè principato nuovo; perchè non e figliuoli del principe vecchio sono eredi e rimangono signori, ma colui che è eletto a quel grado da coloro che ne hanno autorità. Ed essendo questo ordine antiquato, non si può chiamare principato nuovo, perchè in quello non sono alcune di quelle difficultà che sono ne' nuovi; perchè, sebbene el principe è nuovo, li ordini di quello stato sono vecchi, e ordinati a riceverlo come se fussi loro signore ereditario.

Ma torniamo alla materia nostra. Dico che qualunque considerrà el soprascritto discorso, vedrà o l'odio o il disprezzo essere suto cagione della ruina di quelli imperadori prenominati; e conoscerà ancora donde nacque che, parte di loro procedendo in uno modo e parte al contrario, in qualunque di quelli, uno di loro ebbe felice e li altri infelice fine. Perchè a Pertinace ed Alessandro, per essere principi nuovi, fu inutile e dannoso volere imitare Marco che era nel principato iure hereditario; e similmente a Caracalla, Commodo e Massimino essere stata cosa perniziosa imitare Severo, per non avere auta tanta virtù che bastassi a seguitare le vestigie sua. Pertanto, uno principe nuovo, in uno principato nuovo, non può imitare le azioni di Marco, nè ancora è necessario seguitare quelle di Severo; ma debbe pigliare da Severo quelle parti che per fondare el suo stato sono necessarie, e da Marco quelle che sono convenienti e gloriose a conservare uno stato che sia di già stabilito e fermo.

Sultan which is entirely in the hands of the soldiers; he too must, without concern for the people, maintain their friendship. And it should be noted that the state of the Sultan is unlike all other principalities and similar to the Christian pontificate, which cannot be called either a hereditary principality or a new principality, for it is not the sons of the former prince that are the heirs and that remain as lords, but rather that one who is elected to that post by those who have authority. And since this system is an ancient one, the principality cannot be called a new one, for it has none of those difficulties that a new one has; for, although the prince is new, the laws of that state are old and are set up to receive him as though he were their hereditary lord.

But let us return to our subject. Let me say that whoever reflects on the discourse written above will see that either hatred or disdain was the cause of the downfall of the emperors mentioned earlier; and he will also understand how it comes about that, though some acted in one way and some in a contrary way, whatever the way they acted, one came to a prosperous, the others to an unprosperous end. For Pertinax and Alexander, since they were new princes, it was useless and harmful to want to imitate Marcus, who came into power by hereditary right; and likewise for Caracalla, Commodus and Maximinus it was fatal to imitate Severus, since they did not possess enough ingenuity to follow in his footsteps. Therefore, a new prince in a new principality cannot imitate the actions of Marcus, nor is it even necessary for him to follow those of Severus; rather he should take from Severus those qualities which are necessary to establish his own state, and from Marcus those that are suited to its maintenance and glory once the state is already established and secure.

NOTES

1. Especially in Chapter XVI.

2. In Chapter XVII.

3. For the most part in Chapters XV through XIX.

4. Bologna was governed by Santi Bentivogli from the death of Annibale Bentivogli in 1445 until Giovanni came of age in 1462. The latter governed Bologna until he was driven into exile by Julius II in 1506.

5. Parliament.

6. Recall Chapter VII.

7. From 161 A.D. to 238 A.D.

8. Marcus Aurelius, the adopted son of Antonius Pius, was Emperor of Rome from 161 to 180; he maintained justice and order in the Empire and was famous above all as a philosopher.

9. Publius Helvius Pertinax (126–193) was assassinated by the Praetorian Guard shortly after becoming Emperor (from January to March of 193).

10. Emperor of Rome from 222–235. His grandmother (Julia Maesa) and his mother (Julia Mamaea) plotted against the Emperor Heliogabalus. They convinced the Praetorian Guard to kill Heliogabalus and his mother (Julia Soaemias, daughter of Julia Maesa) and proclaim Alexander, who was fourteen years old at the time, Emperor in 222. In spite of the fact that his rule was heavily influenced by his mother (his grandmother passed away shortly after he took the throne) and his tutor, Ulpian, the Empire did prosper under his numerous reforms. In 235, his army turned against him, killing both him and his mother, and made Maximinus emperor.

11. Emperor of Rome from 193 to 211. He weakened the power of the aristocracy and senate, giving more power to the army. He devoted most of his reign to waging war and died a natural death at the age of 65.

12. Chapter XVIII.

13. Marcus Aurelius Antonius Caracalla succeeded Severus as Roman Emperor in 211. He was assassinated by one of his soldiers in 217.

14. Marcus Commodus succeeded his father, Marcus Aurelius, in 180. Marcia, his mistress, and Laetus, the praetorian prefect, conspired against him and had him killed in 193.

15. Caius Julius Verus Maximinus succeeded Alexander

Severus as Emperor of Rome in 235. He was killed by his own legions in 238.

16. Roman Emperor from 218 to 222. As a young priest of Baal he took the name of Heliogabalus, meaning "the creative-god" (see note 10).

17. Emperor from 217 to 218. After the assassination of Caracalla, Macrinus, who was prefect of the Guard, proclaimed himself emperor. Caracalla's aunt, Julia Maesa, had him overthrown in favor of Heliogabalus, her grandson.

18. Marcus Didius Julianus succeeded Pertinax as Emperor of Rome in 193. When Pertinax was killed by the Praetorian Guard, Julianus bought the right to the Empire. He was beheaded after only a few months in office (March 28 to June 2, 193).

Alcuni principi, per tenere securamente lo stato, hanno disarmato e loro sudditi; alcuni altri hanno tenuto divise le terre subiette; alcuni hanno nutrito inimicizie contro a se medesimi; alcuni altri si sono volti a guadagnarsi quelli che li erano suspetti nel principio del suo stato; alcuni hanno edificato fortezze, alcuni le hanno ruinate e destrutte. E benchè di tutte queste cose non si possi dare determinata sentenzia se non si viene a' particulari di quelli stati dove si avessi a pigliare alcuna simile deliberazione, nondimanco io parlerò in quel modo largo che la materia per se medesima sopporta.

Non fu mai, adunque, che uno principe nuovo disarmassi e sua sudditi; anzi, quando gli ha trovati disarmati, sempre gli ha armati; perchè armandosi, quelle arme diventano tua; diventano fedeli quelli che ti sono sospetti, e quelli che erano fedeli si mantengono, e di sudditi si fanno tuoi partigiani. E perchè tutti e sudditi non si possono armare, quando si benefichino quelli che tu armi, con li altri si può fare più a sicurtà; e quella diversità del procedere che conoscono in loro, li fa tua obligati; quelli altri ti scusano, iudicando essere necessario quelli avere più merito che hanno più periculo e più obligo. Ma quando tu li disarmi, tu cominci a offenderli; mostri che tu abbi in loro diffidenzia, o per viltà o per poca fede; e l'una e l'altra di queste opinioni concepe odio contro di te. E perchè tu non puoi stare disarmato, conviene ti volti alla milizia mercenaria, la quale è di quella qualità che di sopra è detto; e quando la fussi buona, la non può essere tanta che ti defenda da' nimici potenti e da' sudditi sospetti. Però, come io ho detto, uno principe nuovo, in uno principato nuovo, sempre vi ha ordinato le armi; e di questi esempli ne sono piene le istorie.

XX   Whether Fortresses and Many Other Things Which Princes Use Frequently Are Useful or Harmful

Some princes, in order to hold on to the state securely, have disarmed their subjects; some others have kept their conquered territories divided into factions; some have cultivated hostilities against their very selves; some others have turned to winning over those who were suspect at the beginning of their reign; some have constructed fortresses; some have torn them down and destroyed them. And even though one cannot formulate a definite precept in regard to all these things without considering the particulars of those states that had to adopt some similar procedure, I shall nevertheless speak in as general terms as the subject will allow.

Now there has never been a time when a new prince has disarmed his subjects; on the contrary, when he has found them disarmed, he has always armed them, because, once armed, those arms become yours; those you find suspicious become loyal; and those who were loyal continue to be so, and from your subjects they become your partisans. But since not all your subjects can be armed, when those you arm are favored, you can deal more safely with the others; and the difference of treatment they recognize on their behalf makes them obliged to you; the others forgive you, judging that those who are subject to more danger and more responsibility must be more deserving. But when you disarm them, you begin to offend them; you show you have no trust in them either out of fear or lack of confidence: and both of these opinions generate hate against you. And since you cannot remain unarmed, you will have to turn to mercenary troops, who are of that caliber mentioned previously; and even if they were good, they could not be strong enough to defend you from powerful enemies and from untrustworthy subjects. So, as I have said, a new

Ma quando uno principe acquista uno stato nuovo che, come membro, si aggiunga al suo vecchio, allora è necessario disarmare quello stato, eccetto quelli che nello acquistarlo sono suti tua partigiani; e quelli ancora, col tempo e con le occasioni, è necessario renderli molli ed effeminati; e ordinarsi in modo che solo le armi di tutto el tuo stato sieno in quelli tua soldati proprii, che nello stato tuo antiquo vivano appresso di te.

Solevano li antiqui nostri, e quelli che erano stimati savii, dire come era necessario tenere Pistoia con le parte e Pisa con le fortezze; e per questo nutrivano in qualche terra loro suddita le differenzie, per possederle più facilmente. Questo, in quelli tempi che Italia era in uno certo modo bilanciata, doveva essere ben fatto; ma non credo già che si possa dare oggi per precetto; perchè io non credo che le divisioni facessero mai bene alcuno; anzi è necessario, quando il nimico si accosta, che le città divise si perdino subito; perchè sempre la parte più debole si aderirà alle forze esterne, e l'altra non potrà reggere.

E Viniziani, mossi, come io credo, dalle ragioni soprascritte, nutrivono le sètte guelfe e ghibelline nelle città loro suddite; e benchè non li lasciassino mai venire al sangue, tamen nutrivono fra loro questi dispareri, acciò che, occupati quelli cittadini in quelle loro differenzie, non si unissino contro di loro. Il che, come si vide, non tornò loro poi a proposito; perchè, sendo rotti a Vailà, subito una parte di quelle prese ardire, e tolsero loro tutto lo stato. Arguiscono, pertanto, simili modi debolezza del principe; perchè in uno principato gagliardo mai si per-

prince in a new principality has always set up an army; and history is full of such examples.

But when a prince acquires a new state that, as a member, is joined to his old one, then it is necessary to disarm that state, except for those who, while it was being acquired, served as your partisans; and even those, in time and when the occasion lends itself, must be rendered weak and effeminate; and things must be arranged in such a way that all of the armed forces of your state consist only of your own soldiers who live close to you in your long-established state.

It was customary for our ancestors, and such among them who were considered wise, to say that it was necessary to hold on to Pistoia by factions and Pisa by fortresses; and for this reason they would cultivate dissension in a number of the towns subject to them, in order to control them more easily. This, during those times when Italy had to some extent a balance of powers, may have been a good thing to do; but I do not believe that it can be offered today as a rule of procedure, because I do not believe that factions ever did anyone any good; indeed, it is inevitable, when the enemy draws near, that the divided cities will be lost at once, for the weaker factions will always join up with the outside forces, and the other will not be able to hold up.

The Venetians, motivated, as I believe, by the reasons mentioned above, cultivated the Guelf and Ghibelline parties[1] in the cities subject to them; and though they never allowed things to come to bloodshed, they nonetheless cultivated these discords between them so that those citizens, occupied with their own differences, would not unite against them. This, as we have seen, did not turn out to their advantage, for, when they were defeated at Vailà, one of those factions quickly got brave and took the entire state from them. Such methods, moreover,

metteranno simili divisioni; perchè le fanno solo profitto a tempo di pace, potendosi, mediante quelle, più facilmente maneggiare e sudditi; ma venendo la guerra, mostra simile ordine la fallacia sua.

Sanza dubbio e principi diventano grandi quando superano le difficultà e le opposizioni che sono fatte loro; e però la fortuna, massime quando vuole fare grande uno principe nuovo, il quale ha maggiore necessità di acquistare reputazione che uno ereditario, li fa nascere de' nimici, e falli fare delle imprese contro, acciò che quello abbi cagione di superarle e, su per quella scala che gli hanno porta e nimici sua, salire più alto. Però molti iudicano che uno principe savio debbe, quando e' ne abbi la occasione, nutrirsi con astuzia qualche inimicizia, acciò che, oppresso quella, ne seguiti maggiore sua grandezza.

Hanno e principi, et praesertim quelli che sono nuovi, trovato più fede e più utilità in quelli uomini che nel principio del loro stato sono suti tenuti sospetti, che in quelli che nel principio erano confidenti. Pandolfo Petrucci, principe di Siena, reggeva lo stato suo più con quelli che li furono sospetti che con gli altri. Ma di questa cosa non si può parlare largamente, perchè la varia secondo el subietto. Solo dirò questo: che quelli uomini, che nel principio di uno principato erono stati inimici, che sono di qualità che a mantenersi abbino bisogno di appoggiarsi, sempre el principe con facilità grandissima se li potrà guadagnare; e loro maggiormente sono forzati a servirlo con fede, quanto conoscano essere loro più necessario cancellare con le opere quella opinione sinistra che si aveva di loro. E così el principe ne trae sempre più utilità, che di coloro che, servendolo con troppa sicurtà, straccurono le cose sua.

indicate weakness in the prince: for in a strong principality such divisions would never be permitted, since they are profitable only in times of peace, allowing the subjects by their means to be controlled more easily; but with the coming of war such a policy shows its fallacy.

Without a doubt princes become great when they overcome the difficulties and oppositions imposed on them; and so fortune, especially when it wants to increase the prestige of a new prince, who has more need of acquiring a reputation than does a hereditary one, creates enemies for him and makes them take action against him, so that he will have reason to overcome them and climb higher up the ladder his enemies have brought him. Therefore many hold that a wise prince, when he has the opportunity, should shrewdly cultivate some hostility, so that, in stamping it out, his greatness is augmented.

Princes, and primarily those who are new, have found more loyalty and usefulness in those men who at the beginning of their reign were held in suspicion than in those who at the beginning were trusted. Pandolfo Petrucci,[2] prince of Siena, governed his state more by means of those who had been suspect than by the others. But about this matter one cannot speak in general terms, because it varies according to the case. I shall say only this: that the prince will always with great ease be able to win over those men who at the start of a principality had been enemies, the kind that in order to maintain themselves must have support; and they are all the more obliged to serve him faithfully inasmuch as they realize the necessity of cancelling, through their deeds, that bad impression he held of them; and in this way the prince will always derive more usefulness from them than from those who, in serving him with too much security, neglect his interests.

E poichè la materia lo ricerca, non voglio lasciare indrieto ricordare a' principi che hanno preso uno stato di nuovo mediante e favori intrinseci di quello, che considerino bene qual cagione abbi mosso quelli che lo hanno favorito, a favorirlo; e se la non è affezione naturale verso di loro, ma fussi solo perchè quelli non si contentavano di quello stato, con fatica e difficultà grande se li potrà mantenere amici, perchè e' fia impossibile che lui possa contentarli. E discorrendo bene, con quelli esempli che dalle cose antiche e moderne si traggano, la cagione di questo, vedrà esserli molto più facile guadagnarsi amici quelli uomini che dello stato innanzi si contentavano, e però erano suoi inimici, che quelli che, per non se ne contentare, li diventorono amici e favironlo a occuparlo.

È suta consuetudine de' principi, per potere tenere più sicuramente lo stato loro, edificare fortezze, che sieno la briglia e il freno di quelli che disegnassino fare loro contro, e avere uno refugio sicuro da uno subito impeto. Io laudo questo modo, perchè gli è usitato ab antiquo; nondimanco, messer Niccolò Vitelli, ne' tempi nostri, si è visto disfare dua fortezze in Città di Castello, per tenere quello stato; Guido Ubaldo, duca di Urbino, ritornato nella sua dominazione donde da Cesare Borgia era suto cacciato, ruinò funditus tutte le fortezze di quella provincia, e iudicò sanza quelle più difficilmente riperdere quello stato; e Bentivogli, ritornati in Bologna, usorono simili termini. Sono, dunque, le fortezze utili o no, secondo e tempi; e se le ti fanno bene in una parte, ti offendano in una altra. E puossi discorrere questa parte così: quel principe che ha più paura de' populi che de' forestieri, debbe fare le fortezze; ma quello che ha più paura de' forestieri che de' populi, debbe lasciarle indrieto. Alla casa sforzesca ha fatto e farà più guerra il castello di Milano, che vi edificò Francesco Sforza, che alcuno altro

And since the subject calls for it, I do not want to fail
to remind princes who have taken over a state recently
by favor of its inhabitants to consider carefully what
reason may have moved these who have favored him to
favor him; and if it is not a natural affection for him,
but merely because they were not satisfied with that state,
only with great struggle and difficulty will he be able to
keep them as friends, because it will be impossible for him
to satisfy them. And examining carefully the cause of
this, with the help of those examples taken from ancient
and modern times, he will see that it is much easier to
win over as friends those men who were satisfied with
the state before, and therefore were his enemies, than
those who, because they were not satisfied with it, became
his friends and helped him to take it over.

It has been customary for princes, in order to hold their
state more securely, to construct fortresses that may serve
as the bridle and bit for those who might plan to attack
them, and to have a safe refuge against a sudden revolt.
I commend this policy, because it was used in ancient
times. Nevertheless, Messer Niccolò Vitelli,[3] in our own
times, was seen to destroy two fortresses in Città di
Castello in order to hold on to that state. Guido Ubaldo,[4]
Duke of Urbino, on returning to his dominion from which
Cesare Borgia had driven him, completely demolished all
the fortresses of that province, and he decided that without them it would be more difficult to recapture that
state. The Bentivogli,[5] when they returned to Bologna,
took similar steps. Fortresses, then, are useful or not according to circumstances; and if they benefit you in one way,
they harm you in another. This matter may be treated as
follows: that prince who is more afraid of the people than
of foreigners should build fortresses; but that one who is
more afraid of foreigners than of the people should not
be concerned with them. The castle of Milan, which

disordine di quello stato. Però la migliore fortezza che sia, è non essere odiato dal populo; perchè, ancora che tu abbi le fortezze, e il populo ti abbi in odio, le non ti salvono; perchè non mancono mai a' populi, preso che gli hanno l'armi, forestieri che li soccorrino. Ne' tempi nostri non si vede che quelle abbino profittato ad alcuno principe, se non alla contessa di Furlì, quando fu morto el conte Girolamo suo consorte; perchè, mediante quella, possè fuggire l'impeto populare e aspettare el soccorso da Milano e recuperare lo stato. E li tempi stavano allora in modo, che il forestiere non posseva soccorrere el populo. Ma di poi valsono ancora a lei poco le fortezze, quando Cesare Borgia l'assaltò e che il populo suo inimico si coniunse col forestiero. Pertanto, allora e prima, sarebbe suto più sicuro a lei non essere odiata dal populo che avere le fortezze.

Considerato, adunque, tutte queste cose, io lauderò chi farà le fortezze e chi non le farà; e biasimerò qualunque, fidandosi delle fortezze, stimerà poco essere odiato da' populi.

NOTES

1. The Guelph and Ghibelline parties in Italy denoted, generally speaking, the party of the Papacy and Italian local independence of the emperor, and the imperialist party, respectively.

2. He ruled Siena from 1500 to 1512 and was Duke Valentino's bitterest enemy as well as his most able adversary.

3. Niccolò Vitelli, a mercenary captain, was made "signore" of the city of Castello by the favor of the Medici. He was driven out by Sixtus IV in 1474 and was able to return only after the Pope's death in 1482. With the help of the Florentines he then destroyed the two fortresses that the Pope had had constructed there.

Francesco Sforza built there, has caused and will cause more war against the House of Sforza than any other disorder in that state. However, the best fortress that exists is not to be hated by the people, because, though you may have fortresses, they will not save you if the people hate you; for once the people have taken up arms, foreigners that will come to their assistance are never scarce. In our own times we have not seen them profit any prince, except the Countess of Furlì[6] when her consort the Count Girolamo was killed; for, by such means, she was able to escape the revolt of the people and wait for help from Milan and regain her state; and the times then were such that a foreigner was not able to give assistance to the people. But then the fortresses were of little avail to her when Cesare Borgia attacked her, and the people, her enemy, joined up with the foreigner. And so, then and before, it would have been safer for her not to have been hated by the people than to have had the fortresses.

Having, then, taken all these things into consideration, I shall commend him who builds fortresses and him who does not build them; and I shall reproach any one who, placing his trust in fortresses, places little value in being hated by the people.

4. Guido Ubaldo of Montefeltro, the Duke of Urbino in 1482, was driven out of there twice by Cesare Borgia, but returned after the death of Alexander VI. He gained possession of Urbino in 1502 and died in 1508.

5. The Bentivogli, expelled from Bologna in 1506 by Julius II, re-entered in 1511.

6. Catherine Sforza, when her husband (Girolamo Riario) was killed in a conspiracy, took refuge in her fortress, and there awaited the aid of Ludovico il Moro, who restored her to her domain, of which she had been deprived in 1500 by Cesare Borgia.

XXI Quod Principem Deceat ut Egregius Habeatur

Nessuna cosa fa tanto stimare uno principe, quanto fanno le grandi imprese e dare di sè rari esempli. Noi abbiamo ne' nostri tempi Ferrando di Aragona, presente re di Spagna. Costui si può chiamare quasi principe nuovo, perchè di uno re debole è diventato, per fama e per gloria, el primo re de' Cristiani; e se considerrete le azioni sua, le troverrete tutte grandissime e qualcuna estraordinaria. Lui, nel principio del suo regno, assaltò la Granata: e quella impresa fu il fondamento dello stato suo. Prima, e' la fece ozioso e sanza sospetto di essere impedito; tenne occupati in quella gli animi di quelli baroni di Castiglia e quali, pensando a quella guerra, non pensavano a innovare; e lui acquistava, in quel mezzo, reputazione e imperio sopra di loro che non se ne accorgevano; possè nutrire, con danari della Chiesa e de' populi, eserciti, e fare uno fondamento, con quella guerra lunga, alla milizia sua; la quale lo ha di poi onorato. Oltre a questo, per potere intraprendere maggiore imprese, servendosi sempre della religione, si volse a una pietosa crudeltà, cacciando e spogliando el suo regno, de' Marrani: nè può essere questo esemplo più miserabile nè più raro. Assaltò, sotto questo medesimo mantello, l'Affrica; fece l'impresa di Italia; ha ultimamente assaltato la Francia. E così sempre ha fatte e ordite cose grande, le quali sempre hanno tenuto sospesi e ammirati gli animi de' sudditi, e occupati nello evento di esse. E sono nate queste sua azioni in modo, l'una dall'altra, che non ha dato mai, infra l'una e l'altra, spazio alli uomini di potere quietamente operarli contro.

XXI   How a Prince Should Act to Acquire Esteem

Nothing makes a prince more esteemed than great enterprises and evidence of his unusual abilities. In our own times we have Ferdinand of Aragon, the present king of Spain. This man can almost be called a new prince, because he rose with fame and glory from a weak king to the foremost king of Christendom; and if you will examine his accomplishments you will find them all very great and some of them extraordinary. Early in his reign he attacked Granada,[1] and that enterprise was the foundation of his state. At first, he carried on the campaign while things were peaceful, without fear of being impeded: he kept the minds of the Barons of Castille[2] occupied with it, and they, concentrating on that war, did not think about changes at home. And he acquired, in the meanwhile, prestige and control over them without their knowing it; he was able, with the money of the church and the people, to support troops and lay a foundation during that long war for his own army; which brought him honor later on. Besides this, to be able to undertake greater enterprises, continuing to make use of religion, he turned to a kind of holy cruelty by chasing out and clearing the Moors from his kingdom:[3] no accomplishment could have been more pathetic or unusual. He attacked, under the same cloak, Africa; he conducted the campaign in Italy; he finally attacked France; and in this way he continuously carried out and contrived great things that always kept the minds of his subjects uncertain and amazed and occupied with the outcome of events. And one action of his would spring from another, so that between one and the other he would never allow enough time for men to work calmly against him.

Giova ancora assai a uno principe dare di sè esempli rari circa e governi di drento, simili a quelli che si narrano di messer Bernabò da Milano, quando si ha l'occasione di qualcuno che operi qualche cosa estraordinaria, o in bene o in male, nella vita civile; e pigliare uno modo circa premiarlo o punirlo, di che s'abbia a parlare assai. E sopra tutto uno principe si debbe ingegnare dare di sè in ogni sua azione fama di uomo grande e d'ingegno eccellente.

È ancora stimato uno principe, quando elli è vero amico e vero inimico; cioè quando, sanza alcuno respetto, si scuopre in favore di alcuno contro ad un altro. Il quale partito fia sempre più utile che stare neutrale; perchè, se dua potenti tuoi vicini vengano alle mani, o e' sono di qualità che, vincendo uno di quelli, tu abbi a temere del vincitore, o no. In qualunque di questi dua casi, ti sarà sempre più utile lo scoprirti e fare buona guerra; perchè, nel primo caso, se tu non ti scuopri, sarai sempre preda di chi vince, con piacere e satisfazione di colui che è stato vinto, e non hai ragione nè cosa alcuna che ti difenda nè che ti riceva; perchè, chi vince non vuole amici sospetti e che non lo aiutino nelle avversità; chi perde, non ti riceve, per non avere tu voluto con le arme in mano correre la fortuna sua.

Era passato in Grecia Antioco, messovi dalli Etoli per cacciarne e Romani. Mandò Antioco oratori alli Achei, che erano amici de' Romani, a confortarli a stare di mezzo; e da altra parte e Romani li persuadevano a pigliare le arme per loro. Venne questa materia a deliberarsi nel concilio delli Achei, dove il legato di Antioco li persuadeva a stare neutrali; a che il legato romano respose:

It is also most helpful for a prince to furnish unusual evidence of his abilities in regard to internal politics, such as we hear told about Messer Bernabò of Milan;[4] when the occasion arises that an individual in civil life performs some extraordinary deed, whether good or bad, he should choose a way of rewarding him or punishing him that will stimulate much discussion. And above all, a prince should strive in all his actions to give the impression of the great man of outstanding intelligence.

A prince is also esteemed when he is a true friend or a true enemy; that is when, without any reservation, he declares himself in favor of one against another. Such a policy will always be more useful than remaining neutral; because if two powerful neighbors of yours come to blows, they will be of the sort that, when one of them has won, you will either have reason to fear the victor, or you will not. In either of these two instances, it will always be more useful for you to declare yourself and fight an open war; for, in the first instance, if you do not declare yourself, you will always be the prey of the winner, to the delight and satisfaction of the one who has been defeated, and you have no excuse, nothing to defend you, nor anyone to offer you refuge; because, whoever wins does not want dubious friends that would not help him in adverse times, and whoever loses will not take you in, since you were not willing to run the risk of coming to his defense.

At the request of the Aetolians, Antiochus moved into Greece to chase out the Romans. Antiochus sent envoys to the Achaeans, who were friendly toward the Romans, to encourage them to remain neutral; and on the other hand the Romans were encouraging them to take up arms on their behalf. This matter came up for consideration in the council of the Achaeans, where the legate of Anti-

« Quod autem isti dicunt non interponendi vos bello, nihil magis alienum rebus vestris est; sine gratia, sine dignitate, praemium victoris eritis ».

E sempre interverrà che colui che non è amico ti ricercherà della neutralità, e quello che ti è amico ti richiederà che ti scuopra con le arme. E li principi mal resoluti, per fuggire e presenti periculi, seguono el più delle volte quella via neutrale, e il più delle volte ruinano. Ma quando el principe si scuopre gagliardamente in favore d' una parte, se colui con chi tu ti aderisci vince, ancora che sia potente e che tu rimanga a sua discrezione, elli ha teco obligo, e vi è contratto l' amore; e li uomini non sono mai sì disonesti, che con tanto esemplo di ingratitudine ti opprimessero; di poi, le vittorie non sono mai sì stiette, che il vincitore non abbi ad avere qualche respetto, e messime alla giustizia. Ma se quello con il quale tu ti aderisci perde, tu se' ricevuto da lui; e mentre che può ti aiuta, e diventi compagno d' una fortuna che può resurgere.

Nel secondo caso, quando quelli che combattono insieme sono di qualità che tu non abbi a temere di quello che vince, tanto è maggiore prudenzia lo aderirsi, perchè tu vai alla ruina di uno con lo aiuto di chi lo doverrebbe salvare, se fussi savio; e, vincendo, rimane a tua discrezione, ed è impossibile, con lo aiuto tuo, che non vinca.

E qui è da notare che uno principe debbe avvertire di non fare mai compagnia con uno più potente di sè per offendere altri, se non quando la necessità lo stringe, come di sopra si dice; perchè, vincendo, rimani suo prigione: e li principi debbano fuggire, quanto possono, lo stare a

ochus persuaded them to remain neutral; whereupon the Roman legate replied: "The advice these people give you about not getting mixed up in a war is indeed contrary to your interests; without respect, without dignity, you will be the prey of the victors."

And it will always happen that he who is not your friend will request your neutrality, and that one who is your friend will ask you to declare yourself by taking up arms. And the irresolute princes, in order to flee present dangers, most often follow the neutral road, and most often they ruin themselves. But when a prince undauntedly declares himself in favor of one side, if the one with whom you join wins, though he may be powerful and you may be left to his discretion, he is in your debt and a bond of friendship exists; and men are never so dishonest as to turn on you with such obvious ingratitude; and then, victories are never so clear-cut that the victor need not show some caution, especially with justice. But if the one with whom you join loses, you will be taken in by him; and while he is able he will assist you, and you become the companion of a fortune that may spring up again.

In the second case, when those who are fighting each other are of the caliber that you need not fear the one who wins, it is all the more wise for you to join sides, because you attend the downfall of one with the help of the other who should have saved him, if he had been wise; and in winning he is left to your discretion, and it is impossible for him with your help not to win.

And here it is to be noted that a prince should be careful never to join forces with one more powerful than himself against others unless necessity demands it, as was mentioned above; for, in winning, you are his prisoner; and princes should avoid, as much as possible, being left

discrezione di altri. E Viniziani si accompagnorno con Francia contro al duca di Milano; e potevono fuggire di non fare quella compagnia; di che ne resultò la ruina loro. Ma quando non si può fuggirla (come intervenne a' Fiorentini quando il papa e Spagna andorono con li eserciti ad assaltare la Lombardia) allora si debba el principe aderire per le ragioni sopradette. Nè creda mai alcuno stato potere sempre pigliare partiti securi, anzi pensi di avere a prenderli tutti dubii; perchè si truova questo nell' ordine delle cose, che mai non si cerca fuggire uno inconveniente che non si incorra in uno altro; ma la prudenzia consiste in sapere conoscere le qualità delli inconvenienti, e pigliare el meno tristo per buono.

Debbe ancora uno principe mostrarsi amatore delle virtù, dando recapito alli uomini virtuosi e onorando gli eccellenti in una arte. Appresso, debbe animare li sua cittadini di potere quietamente esercitare li esercizii loro, e nella mercantia e nella agricultura e in ogni altro esercizio delli uomini; e che quello non tema di ornare le sua possessione per timore che le gli sieno tolte, e quell' altro di aprire uno traffico per paura delle taglie; ma debbe preparare premii a chi vuol fare queste cose, e a qualunque pensa in qualunque modo ampliare la sua città o il suo stato. Debbe, oltre a questo, ne' tempi convenienti dell' anno, tenere occupati e populi con le feste e spettaculi. E perchè ogni città è divisa in arte o in tribù, debbe tenere conto di quelle università, raunarsi con loro qualche volta, dare di sè esemplo di umanità e di munificenzia, tenendo sempre ferma nondimanco la maestà della dignità sua, perchè questo non vuole mai mancare in cosa alcuna.

to the mercy of others. The Venetians joined up with France against the Duke of Milan, and they could have avoided making such an alliance, which resulted in their downfall. But when it cannot be avoided (as happened to the Florentines when the Pope and Spain led their armies in the assault against Lombardy) then a prince should join a side for the reasons mentioned above. Nor let any state ever believe that it can always adopt safe policies, rather let it think that they will all be uncertain; for this is what we find to be in the order of things: that we never try to escape one difficulty without running into another; but prudence consists in knowing how to recognize the nature of the difficulties and how to choose the least bad as good.

Furthermore a prince should show that he is an admirer of talent by giving recognition to talented men, and honoring those who excel in a particular art. Moreover, he should encourage his subjects to enable them to pursue their trades in tranquility, whether they be in commerce, agriculture, or any other trade a man may have; so that one man will not be afraid to enrich his possessions for fear that they will be taken from him, while another will not be afraid to engage in commerce through fear of taxes; rather he should establish awards for those who wish to do these things and for whoever seeks in any way to aggrandize his city or his state. He should, besides this, at appropriate times during the year, keep the people occupied with festivals and shows. And since every city is divided into guilds or clans, he should keep these groups in mind, meet with them at times, give evidence of his kindness and munificence, always maintaining firmly, however, the dignity of his position, for this should never be lacking in any way.

NOTES

1. He was victorious against the Moors on February 4, 1492.

2. These barons were bitter about losing their independence when Castille was united to Aragon through the marriage of Isabella and Ferdinand.

3. The Moors were finally expelled from Spain in 1501–2.

4. Bernabò Visconti, Lord of Milan from 1354 to 1385, was noted for his cruelty and peculiarity, but admired for his political wisdom and energy, his organization of actions and intentions, and his vigorous unitarian impulse expressed in Visconti politics. His bizarre methods of punishing became legendary.

Non è di poca importanzia a uno principe la elezione de'
ministri; e quali sono buoni o no, secondo la prudenzia
del principe. E la prima coniettura che si fa del cervello
di uno signore, è vedere li uomini che lui ha d'intorno;
e quando e' sono sufficienti e fedeli, si può sempre repu-
tarlo savio, perchè ha saputo conoscerli sufficienti e mantenerli fedeli; ma quando sieno altrimenti, sempre si può
fare non buono iudizio di lui; perchè el primo errore che
fa, lo fa in questa elezione.

Non era alcuno che conoscessi messer Antonio da
Venafro per ministro di Pandolfo Petrucci principe di
Siena, che non iudicassi Pandolfo essere valentissimo
uomo, avendo quello per suo ministro. E perchè sono di
tre generazione cervelli: l'uno intende da sè, l'altro dis-
cerne quello che altri intende, el terzo non intende nè
sè nè altri; quel primo è eccellentissimo, el secondo eccellente, el terzo inutile; conveniva pertanto di necessità
che, se Pandolfo non era nel primo grado, che fussi nel
secondo; perchè, ogni volta che uno ha iudicio di conoscere el bene o il male che uno fa e dice, ancora che da
sè non abbia invenzione, conosce l'opere triste e le buone
del ministro e quelle esalta e le altre corregge; e il ministro non può sperare d'ingannarlo e mantiensi buono.

Ma come uno principe possa conoscere il ministro, ci
è questo modo che non falla mai. Quando tu vedi el
ministro pensare più a sè che a te, e che in tutte le azioni
vi recerca drento l'utile suo, questo tale così fatto mai
fia buono ministro, mai te ne potrai fidare; perchè quello
che ha lo stato di uno in mano, non debbe pensare mai
a sè, ma sempre al principe, e non li ricordare mai cosa

XXII   On the Private Counselors a Prince Has

The choosing of ministers is of no little importance to a prince: they are good or not, according to the wisdom of the prince. The first thing one does to evaluate the intelligence of a ruler is to examine the men he has around him; and when they are capable and loyal, he can always be considered wise, for he has known how to recognize their capability and maintain their loyalty. But when they are otherwise, one can always form an unfavorable opinion of him in all other things; because the first mistake he makes, he makes in this choice of ministers.

There was no one who knew Messer Antonio da Venafro[1] as minister of Pandolfo Petrucci,[2] prince of Siena, who did not consider Pandolfo a most clever man for having him as his minister. And since there are three types of intelligence: one understands on its own, another perceives what others understand, the third does not understand either on its own or through others; the first type is more than excellent, the second excellent, the third useless; therefore it must have been that, if Pandolfo was not in the first class, he was in the second: because, whenever one has the intelligence to recognize the good or the evil that one does and says, though he may have no real insight of his own, he, in turn, recognizes the good and the bad deeds of the minister, and is able to praise the one and correct the other; and the minister cannot hope to deceive him and so continues to be good.

But so that a prince may be able to know the minister, there is this method that never fails. When you see the minister thinking more about himself than about you, and that in all his actions he seeks his own interest, such a one as this will never be a good minister, never will you be able to trust him: because he who has another's state in his hands must never think of himself, but of

che non appartenga a lui. E dall' altro canto el principe, per mantenerlo buono, debba pensare al ministro, onorandolo, faccendolo ricco, obligandoselo, partecipandoli li onori ed e carichi, acciò che vegga che non può stare sanza lui, e che gli assai onori non li faccino desiderare più onore, le assai ricchezze non li faccino desiderare più ricchezze, gli assai carichi li faccino temere le mutazioni. Quando, dunque, e ministri, e li principi circa e ministri, sono così fatti, possono confidare l' uno dell'altro; e quando altrimenti, sempre il fine fia dannoso o per l' uno o per l' altro.

the prince, and never be concerned with anything that does not pertain to him. And on the other side, the prince, in order to keep him good, should think of the minister, honoring him, making him rich, putting him in his debt, sharing with him the honors and the duties; so that he may come to see that he cannot get along without the prince, and so that his many honors will not make him desire more honors, his many riches will not make him desire more riches, his many duties will make him fear changes. When, therefore, ministers and princes in relation to ministers are so organized, they can have confidence in one another; and when it is otherwise, the end result will always be disastrous either for the one or the other.

NOTES

1. Antonio da Venafro (Antonio Giordani, born at Venafro in 1459) was a jurist and a diplomat, and taught law at the Studio di Siena.

2. Ruled Siena in 1487 with his brother Giacopo, and in 1497, with the death of his brother and through a number of cruel deeds (he did away with his rivals, including his father-in-law, Niccolò Borghese), he became prince of Siena.

Non voglio lasciare indrieto uno capo importante e uno errore dal quale e principi con difficultà si difendano, se non sono prudentissimi, o se non hanno buona elezione. E questi sono li adulatori, de' quali le corti sono piene; perchè li uomini si compiacciano tanto nelle cose loro proprie, e in modo vi si ingannano, che con difficultà si difendano da questa peste; e a volersene defendere, si porta periculo di non diventare contennendo. Perchè non ci è altro modo a guardarsi dalle adulazione, se non che gli uomini intendino che non ti offendino a dirti el vero; ma quando ciascuno può dirti el vero, ti manca la reverenzia. Pertanto, uno principe prudente debbe tenere uno terzo modo, eleggendo nel suo stato uomini savii, e solo a quelli debbe dare libero arbitrio a parlarli la verità, e di quelle cose sole che lui domanda, e non d'altro. Ma debbe domandarli d'ogni cosa, e le opinioni loro udire e, di poi, deliberare da sè, a suo modo; e con questi consigli e con ciascuno di loro portarsi in modo che ognuno conosca che, quanto più liberamente si parlerà, tanto più li fia accetto; fuora di quelli, non volere udire alcuno, andare drieto alla cosa deliberata ed essere ostinato nelle deliberazioni sua. Chi fa altrimenti, o e' precipita per li adulatori, o si muta spesso per la variazione de' pareri: di che ne nasce la poca estimazione sua.

Io voglio, a questo proposito, addurre uno esemplo moderno. Pre' Luca, uomo di Massimiliano presente imperadore, parlando di sua maestà, disse come e' non si consigliava con persona, e non faceva mai di alcuna cosa a suo modo; il che nasceva dal tenere contrario termine al sopradetto. Perchè lo imperadore è uomo secreto, non comunica li sua disegni con persona, non ne piglia parere;

XXIII *How Flatterers Are to Be Avoided*

I do not want to skip over an important subject and an error from which princes protect themselves with difficulty, if they are not very clever, or do not make good choices. And these are the flatterers, of which courts are full; because men take such delight in their own affairs and in this way deceive themselves, that with difficulty do they defend themselves from this pestilence; and the desire to defend themselves from it brings with it the danger of becoming despised. For there is no other way to guard oneself from flatterers than by letting men know that you will not be offended by being told the truth; but when everyone is able to tell you the truth, you lose their respect. Therefore a wise prince should adopt a third means, choosing wise men for his state, and only to those should he allow the freedom to speak truthfully to him, and only concerning those matters about which he asks, and nothing else. But he should ask them about everything, and listen to their opinions, and afterward deliberate by himslf, in his own way; and with these councils, and with each one of his advisers, he should act in such a way that everyone may know that the more freely he speaks, all the more he will be acceptable: aside from these, he should not want to hear any others, he should carry through what was decided and be firm in his decisions. Who does otherwise either falls prey to the flatterers, or changes his mind many times with the divergence of opinions: because of this he has little esteem.

I wish in this respect to cite a recent example. Father Luca,[1] a follower of Maximilian, the present emperor, speaking of his majesty told how he never sought anyone's advice, yet he never did anything the way he wanted to: this arose from maintaining a position contrary to the one mentioned above. Since the emperor is a secretive man, he discusses his plans with no one, he accepts no

ma come, nel metterli ad effetto, si cominciono a conoscere e scoprire, li cominciono ad essere condradetti da
coloro che lui ha d'intorno; e quello, come facile, se ne
stoglie. Di qui nasce che quelle cose che fa uno giorno,
destrugge l'altro; e che non si intenda mai quello si voglia
o disegni fare; e che non si può sopra le sua deliberazioni
fondarsi.

Uno principe, pertanto, debbe consigliarsi sempre, ma
quando lui vuole e non quando vuole altri; anzi debbe
torre animo a ciascuno di consigliarlo d'alcuna cosa, se
non gnene domanda. Ma lui debbe bene essere largo
domandatore, e di poi, circa le cose domandate, paziente
auditore del vero; anzi, intendendo che alcuno per alcuno
respetto non gnene dica, turbarsene. E perchè molti esis-
timano che alcuno principe, el quale da di sè opinione
di prudente, sia così tenuto non per sua natura ma per
li buoni consigli che lui ha d'intorno, sanza dubbio s'
ingannano. Perchè questa è una regola generale che non
falla mai: che uno principe, il quale non sia savio per se
stesso, non può essere consigliato bene, se già a sorte non
si rimettessi in uno solo che al tutto lo governassi, che
fussi uomo prudentissimo. In questo caso, potria bene
essere, ma durerebbe poco; perchè quello governatore in
breve tempo li torrebbe lo stato. Ma consigliandosi con
più d'uno, uno principe che non sia savio non arà mai
e consigli uniti, nè saprà per se stesso unirli; de' consiglieri,
ciascuno penserà alla proprietà sua; lui non li saprà correggere nè conoscere. E non si possono trovare altrimenti;
perchè li uomini sempre ti riusciranno tristi, se da una
necessità non sono fatti buoni. Però si conclude che li
buoni consigli, da qualunque venghino, conviene naschino
dalla prudenzia del principe, e non la prudenzia del principe da' buoni consigli.

opinions concerning them; but as they begin to be known
and discovered when they are being put into effect, they
begin to be contradicted by those around him; and he,
easily influenced, is diverted from them. From this it
comes about that things he accomplishes one day, he
destroys the next, and that no one ever understands what
he wishes or plans to do, and that one cannot rely on his
decisions.

A prince, therefore, should always seek advice, but only
when he wishes and not when others wish it; indeed, he
should discourage everyone from giving him advice on
any subject, unless he asks for it. Nevertheless he should
certainly be a free asker-of-questions, and afterward, about
what was asked, a patient listener to the truth; moreover,
if he becomes aware that anyone, for whatever reason, is
not telling him the truth, he should become angry. And
since many believe that any prince who gives the appearance of being clever is regarded so not because of his own
merits but because of the good counselors he has around
him, they are without a doubt deceiving themselves. For
here is a general rule that never fails: that a prince who
is not wise in his own right cannot be advised well, unless
purely by chance he submitted himself to a single individual who governed him in all and who was a very wise
man. In this case, he certainly could be, but it would not
last long, because that governor in a short time would
take his state from him. But by seeking advice from more
than one, a prince who is not wise will never have consistent advice, nor will he know how to make it consistent
on his own; all of the counselors will think of their own
interests; he will not know how to manage or understand
them. And it is not possible to find counselors who are
otherwise, for men always turn out badly for you, unless
by some necessity they are made to be good. And so it

may be concluded that good advice, from whomever it may come, must originate from the wisdom of the prince, and not the wisdom of the prince from good advisers.

NOTES

1. Luca Rainaldi was ambassador to the Emperor Maximilian of Germany, whom Machiavelli knew during his legation to the Emperor.

Le cose soprascritte, osservate prudentemente, fanno parere, uno principe nuovo, antico e lo rendono subito più sicuro e più fermo nello stato, che se vi fussi antiquato drento. Perchè uno principe nuovo è molto più osservato nelle sua azioni che uno ereditario; e quando le sono conosciute virtuose, pigliano molto più li uomini e molto più gli obligano che il sangue antico. Perchè li uomini sono molto più presi dalle cose presenti che dalle passate; e quando nelle presenti truovono il bene, vi si godono e non cercono altro; anzi piglieranno ogni difesa per lui, quando non manchi nelle altre cose a sè medesimo. E così arà duplicata gloria: di avere dato principio a uno principato nuovo, e ornatolo e corroboratolo di buone legge, di buone arme e di buoni esempli; come quello ha duplicata vergogna, che, nato principe, lo ha per sua poca prudenzia perduto.

E se si considerrà quelli signori che in Italia hanno perduto lo stato a' nostri tempi, come il re di Napoli, duca di Milano e altri, si troverrà in loro, prima, uno comune defetto quanto alle armi, per le cagioni che di sopra a lungo si sono discorse; di poi, si vedrà alcuno di loro o che arà avuto inimici e populi, o, se arà avuto el populo amico, non si sarà saputo assicurare de' grandi; perchè, sanza questi difetti, non si perdono li stati che abbino tanto nervo che possino trarre uno esercito alla campagna. Filippo Macedone, non il padre di Alessandro, ma quello che fu vinto da Tito Quinto, aveva non molto stato, respetto alla grandezza de' Romani e di Grecia che lo assaltò; nondimanco, per essere uomo militare e che sapeva intrattenere el populo e asicurarsi de' grandi, sostenne più anni la guerra contro a quelli; e se alla fine

XXIV Why the Princes of Italy Have Lost Their States

The things mentioned above, if observed carefully, make a new prince appear long-established and immediately render him more secure and more firm in his state, as though he had aged within it. For the actions of a new prince are more closely observed than those of the hereditary prince; and when they are recognized as good actions, they win men over and hold them in allegiance much better than ancient blood. For men are much more taken by things of the present than of the past; and when they find the present good, they enjoy it and seek nothing else; indeed, they will take every measure to defend the new prince, as long as he is not lacking in his other duties. And so he will have a twofold glory: to have given rise to a new principality, and to have adorned and fortified it with good laws, good arms and good deeds; just as that one will have twofold shame who, born a prince, loses his principality through his meager wisdom.

And if we take into consideration those leaders in Italy who have lost the state in our time, such as the king of Naples,[1] the Duke of Milan,[2] and others, we will find in them, first of all, a common fault with regard to arms, for reasons previously discussed at length;[3] then we will see that some of them either had the people as their enemy or, if they had the people for friends, they did not know how to protect themselves against the nobles: because, without these faults, states are not lost that have enough power to bring an army to the battlefield. Philip of Macedon, not the father of Alexander but the one who was vanquished by Titus Quintius,[4] did not possess much of a state, compared to the greatness of the Romans and of Greece which attacked him; nevertheless, being a military man who knew how to hold on to the people

perdè il dominio di qualche città, li rimase nondimanco el regno.

Pertanto, questi nostri principi, che erano stati molti anni nel principato loro, per averlo di poi perso non accusino la fortuna, ma la ignavia loro: perchè, non avendo mai, ne' tempi quieti, pensato che possono mutarsi (il che è comune defetto delli uomini, non fare conto, nella bonaccia, della tempesta), quando poi vennono e tempi avversi, pensorno a fuggirsi e non a defendersi; e sperororono che e populi, infastiditi dalla insolenzia de' vincitori, gli richiamassino. Il quale partito, quando mancono li altri, è buono; ma è bene male avere lasciati li altri remedii per quello; perchè non si vorrebbe mai cadere per credere di trovare chi ti ricolga; il che, o non avviene, o, s' egli avviene, non è con tua sicurtà, per essere quella difesa suta vile e non dependere da te. E quelle difese solamente sono buone, sono certe, sono durabili, che dependano da te proprio e dalla virtù tua.

and protect himself against the nobles, he waged war against them for many years; and if at the end he lost possession of several cities, he was still left with his kingdom.

Therefore, let these princes of ours who have been in their principalities for many years and then come to lose them not blame fortune, but rather their own laziness: because, never having thought during peaceful times that conditions could change (which is a common fault with men, not to consider the possibility of a storm when the weather is fine), when adverse times then came, they thought about running away instead of defending themselves; and they hoped that the people, disgusted with the outrages of the conquerors, might call them back. Such a measure, when there are no others, is good; but it is certainly bad to have disregarded other remedies for that one; for no one should ever want to fall because he believes he will find someone to pick him up; for whether this happens or not, it does not add to your security, for that method was cowardly and did not depend on your own doing. And those methods alone are good, are certain, are lasting, that depend on you yourself and on your own ingenuity.

NOTES

1. Frederick of Aragon was deprived of his kingdom by the armies of Ferdinand of Spain and Louis XII.

2. Ludovico il Moro was driven out by the armies of Louis XII in 1499.

3. See Chapters XIII and XIV.

4. Roman Consul (198 B.C.), he defeated Philip II of Macedon in 197 B.C. during the second Macedonian War.

XXV *Quantum Fortuna in Rebus Humanis Possit, et Quomodo Illi Sit Occurrendum*

E' non mi è incognito come molti hanno avuto e hanno opinione che le cose del mondo sieno in modo governate dalla fortuna e da Dio, che li uomini con la prudenzia loro non possino correggerle, anzi non vi abbino remedio alcuno; e per questo potrebbano iudicare che non fussi da insudare molto nelle cose, ma lasciarsi governare alla sorte. Questa opinione è suta più creduta ne' nostri tempi, per la variazione grande delle cose che si sono viste e veggonsi ogni dì, fuora di ogni umana coniettura. A che pensando io qualche volta, mi sono in qualche parte inclinato nella opinione loro. Nondimanco, perchè il nostro libero arbitrio non sia spento, iudico potere essere vero che la fortuna sia arbitra della metà delle azioni nostre, ma che etiam lei ne lasci governare l'altra metà, o preso, a noi. E assomiglio quella a uno di questi fiumi rovinosi, che, quando s'adirano, allagano e piani, ruinano gli alberi e gli edifizii, lievano da questa parte terreno, pongono da quell'altra; ciascuno fugge loro dinanzi, ognuno cede allo impeto loro, sanza potervi in alcuna parte obstare. E benchè sieno così fatti, non resta però che li uomini, quando sono tempi quieti, non vi potessino fare provvedimenti e con ripari e argini, in modo che, crescendo poi, o egli andrebbano per uno canale, o l'impeto loro non sarebbe nè si licenzioso nè sì dannoso. Similmente interviene della fortuna; la quale dimostra la sua potenzia dove non è ordinata virtù a resisterle; e quivi volta e sua impeti dove la sa che non sono fatti li argini e li ripari a tenerla. E se voi considerrete la Italia, che è la sedia di queste variazioni e quella che ha dato loro il moto, vedrete essere una campagna sanza argini e sanza alcuno riparo: chè, s'ella fussi riparata da conveniente virtù, come la Magna, la Spagna e la Francia, o questa piena non arebbe fatte le variazioni grande che ha, o la non ci

XXV How Much Fortune Can Do in Human Affairs and How to Contend with It

I am not unaware that many have been and still are of the opinion that worldly affairs are in a way governed by fortune and by God, that men with their wisdom are not able to control them, indeed, that men can do nothing about them; and for this reason they would conclude that there is no point in sweating much over these things, instead let them be governed by chance. This opinion has been held more in our own day, because of the great changes in things that have been observed and are being observed every day that are beyond human imagination. When I think about this sometimes, I am to some extent inclined toward their opinion. Nevertheless, so that our free choice may not be obliterated, I hold that it could be true that fortune is the arbiter of half our actions, but that she still leaves the other half, or close to it, to be governed by us. And she resembles one of those violent rivers that, when they become enraged, flood the plains, tear down trees and buildings, lift up the earth from one side and deposit it on the other; everyone flees before them, everybody yields to their impact, unable to oppose them in any way. And although they are this way, it does not mean therefore that men, when times are quiet, cannot take precautions with floodgates and embankments, so that, when they swell up again, either they would move along through a canal, or their rush would not be so unchecked or so harmful. The same happens with fortune, who displays her force where there is no prepared resource to resist her; and she directs her impact there where she knows that floodgates and banks have not been constructed to contain her. And if you consider Italy, which is the seat of these changes and the one that put them into motion, you will see that she is a country without embankments and without any floodgates: for if

sarebbe venuta. E questo voglio basti avere detto quanto allo opporsi alla fortuna, in universali.

Ma restringendomi più al particulare, dico come si vede oggi questo principe felicitare, e domani ruinare, sanza averli veduto mutare natura o qualità alcuna. Il che credo che nasca, prima, dalle cagioni che si sono lungamente per lo adrieto discorse, cioè che quel principe che si appoggia tutto in su la fortuna, rovina, come quella varia; credo ancora che sia felice quello che riscontra el modo del procedere suo con le qualità de' tempi, e similmente sia infelice quello che con il procedere suo si discordono e tempi. Perchè si vede li uomini, nelle cose che li conducono al fine quale ciascuno ha innanzi, cioè gloria e ricchezze, procedervi variamente; l'uno con respetto, l'altro con impeto; l'uno per violenzia, l'altro con arte; l'uno per pazienzia, l'altro con il suo contrario; e ciascuno con questi diversi modi vi può pervenire. E vedesi ancora dua respettivi, l'uno pervenire al suo disegno, l'altro no; e similmente dua equalmente felicitare con dua diversi studii, sendo l'uno respettivo e l'altro impetuoso; il che non nasce da altro, se non dalla qualità de' tempi che si conformano o no col procedere loro. Di qui nasce quello ho detto, che dua, diversamente operando, sortiscono el medesimo effetto; e dua equalmente operando, l'uno si conduce al suo fine e l'altro no. Da questo ancora depende la variazione del bene; perchè, se uno che si governa con respetti e pazienzia, e tempi e le cose girono in modo che il governo suo sia buono, e' viene felicitando; ma se li tempi e le cose si mutano, e' rovina, perchè non muta modo di procedere. Nè si truova uomo sì prudente che si sappi accomodare a questo; sì perchè non si può deviare da quello a che la natura lo

she had been protected with suitable resources,[1] like Germany, Spain and France, either this flood would not have caused the great changes it has, or it would not have come about at all. And let what I have just said suffice as a general discussion on opposing fortune.

But confining myself more to particulars, let me say that we may see a prince prosper today, and tomorrow come to ruin, without having seen a change in his character or in anything else. This I believe stems, first, from the causes discussed at length earlier; that is, that a prince who relies entirely on fortune will come to ruin as soon as she changes. I believe, furthermore, that he will prosper who adapts his course of action to conditions of the present time, and similarly that he will not prosper who with his course of action conflicts with the times. For men can be seen, in the things which lead them to the goal that each has before him, namely, glory and wealth, to proceed in different ways: one with cautiousness, another with impetuousness; one by violence, another with strategy; one by patience, another by way of its contrary; and each one by these diverse methods can arrive at his goal. Moreover, in the case of two cautious men, we can see one carry out his plan, the other not; and likewise two men prospering equally well by means of two different methods, one being cautious and the other impetuous: which stems from nothing else if not from the conditions of the times that do or do not conform to their course of action. From this arises what I have said, that two men, working in different ways, can produce the same effect; and two men working in the same way, one achieves his goal, and the other does not. From this depends also the mutability of what is good; for, if a man governs himself with caution and patience, and the times and circumstances are in accord so that his course of procedure is good, he will go along prospering; but, if times

inclina; si etiam perchè, avendo sempre uno prosperato camminando per una via, non si può persuadere partirsi da quella. E però l' uomo respettivo, quando egli è tempo di venire allo impeto, non lo sa fare; donde e' rovina; che se si mutassi di natura con li tempi e con le cose, non si muterebbe fortuna.

Papa Iulio II procedè in ogni sua cosa impetuosamente; e trovò tanto e tempi e le cose conforme a quello suo modo di procedere, che sempre sortì felice fine. Considerate la prima impresa che fe', di Bologna, vivendo ancora messer Giovanni Bentivogli. E Viniziani non se ne contentavano; el re di Spagna, quel medesimo; con Francia aveva ragionamenti di tale impresa; e lui nondimanco, con la sua ferocia e impeto, si mosse personalmente a quella espedizione. La quale mossa fece stare sospesi e fermi Spagna e Viniziani; quelli per paura, e quell' altro per il desiderio aveva di recuperare tutto el regno di Napoli; e dall' altro canto si tirò drieto el re di Francia, perchè, vedutolo quel re mosso, e desiderando farselo amico per abbassare e Viniziani, iudicò non poterli negare le sua gente sanza iniuriarlo manifestamente. Condusse adunque Iulio, con la sua mossa impetuosa, quello che mai altro pontefice, contutta la umana prudenzia, arebbe condotto; perchè, se elli aspettava di partirsi da Roma con le conclusione ferme e tutte le cose ordinate, come qualunque altro pontefice arebbe fatto, mai li riusciva; perchè il re di Francia arebbe avuto mille scuse, e li altri messo mille paure. Io voglio lasciare stare le altre sue azioni, che tutte sono state simile, e tutte li sono successe bene; e la brevità della vita non li ha lasciato sentire il

and circumstances change, he is ruined, because he does not change his course of action. Nor does one find a man wise enough to know how to adapt himself to this; not only because he cannot deviate from that to which he is naturally inclined, but also because, having always prospered while following along one path, he cannot be persuaded to leave it. And therefore the cautious man, when it is time for him to act with impetuousness, does not know how; and so he is ruined; for, if he were to change his nature with the times and the circumstances, his fortune would not change.

Pope Julius II in all his dealings acted impetuously; and he found the times and the circumstances very much in accord with his course of action, which always produced favorable results. Consider the first battle he waged, against Bologna, while Messer Giovanni Bentivogli was still alive. The Venetians were not happy about it, and neither was the king of Spain; he was negotiating with France over the enterprise; and nonetheless, with his fierceness and impetuousness, he personally put that campaign into motion. Such a motion kept Spain and the Venetians in check and in place, the latter out of fear, and the other by the desire to regain all the kingdom of Naples; at the same time he drew the king of France into it, because the king, having seen him make this move, and desiring to make him a friend in order to defeat the Venetians, decided he could not deny him his troops without obviously offending him. And so Julius accomplished, with his impetuous move, what no other pontiff, possessing all human wisdom, could accomplish; for, if he had waited to leave Rome until the agreements were established and everything was settled, as any other pontiff would have done, he would never have succeeded; because the king of France would have found a thousand excuses, and the others would have instilled in him a

contrario; perchè, se fussino venuti tempi che fussi biso-
gnato procedere con respetti, ne seguiva la sua ruina: nè
mai arebbe deviato da quelli modi a' quali la natura lo
inclinava.

Concludo adunque, che, variando la fortuna e stando
li uomini ne' loro modi ostinati, sono felici mentre con-
cordano insieme, e, come discordano, infelici. Io iudico
bene questo: che sia meglio essere impetuoso che respettivo; perchè la fortuna è donna, ed è necessario, volendola tenere sotto, batterla e urtarla. E si vede che la si
lascia più vincere da questi, che da quelli che freddamente
procedono; e però sempre, come donna, è amica de' giovanni, perchè sono meno respettivi, più feroci e con più
audacia la comandano.

thousand fears. I want to leave aside his other deeds, for all of them were similar, and all of them turned out well. And the brevity of life did not allow him to experience the opposite; because, if such times had come that might have required him to act with caution, his ruin would have followed from it: for never would he have deviated from those methods to which nature inclined him.

I conclude, then, that fortune varying, and men remaining fixed in their ways, while the two are in accordance with each other men are prosperous, and when they are in discord, unprosperous. I am certainly convinced of this: that it is better to be impetuous than cautious, because fortune is a woman, and it is necessary, if one wishes to hold her down, to beat her and fight with her. And we see that she allows herself to be taken over more by these men than by those who make cold advances; and then, being a woman, she is always the young man's friend, because they are less cautious, more reckless and with greater audacity command her.

NOTES

1. That is, military forces.

XXVI *Exhortatio Ad Capessendam Italiam in Libertatemque a Barbaris Vindicandam*

Considerato, adunque, tutte le cose di sopra discorse, e pensando meco medesimo se, al presente, in Italia correvono tempi da onorare uno nuovo principe, e se ci era materia che dessi occasione a uno prudente e virtuoso di introdurvi forma che facesi onore a lui e bene alla università delli uomini di quella, mi pare concorrino tante cose in benefizio di uno principe nuovo, che io non so qual mai tempo fussi più atto a questo. E se, come io dissi, era necessario, volendo vedere la virtù di Moisè, che il populo d'Isdrael fussi stiavo in Egitto, e, a connoscere la grandezza dello animo di Ciro, ch' e Persi fussino oppressati da' Medi, e la eccellenzia di Teseo, che li Ateniesi fussino dispersi; così, al presente, volendo conoscere la virtù di uno spirito italiano, era necessario che la Italia si riducessi nel termine che ella è di presente: e che la fussi più stiava che gli Ebrei, più serva ch' e Persi, più dispersa che gli Ateniesi; sanza capo, sanza ordine, battuta, spogliata, lacera, corsa, e avessi sopportato d'ogni sorte ruina.

E benchè fino a qui si sia mostro qualche spiraculo in qualcuno, da potere iudicare che fussi ordinato da Dio per sua redenzione, tamen si è visto, da poi, come, nel più alto corso delle azioni sue, è stato dalla fortuna reprobato. In modo che, rimasa come sanza vita, espetta qual possa essere quello che sani le sue ferite, e ponga fine a' sacchi di Lombardia, alle taglie del Reame e di Toscana, e la guarisca di quelle sue piaghe già per lungo tempo infistolite. Vedesi come la prega Dio che le mandi qualcuno che la redima da queste crudeltà ed insolenzie barbare; vedesi ancora tutta pronta e disposta a seguire una bandiera, pur che ci sia uno che la pigli. Nè ci si vede,

XXVI *Exhortation to Take Hold of Italy and Liberate Her from the Barbarians*

So, having deliberated on all the things discussed above, and meditating over whether the time is right in Italy, at present, to honor a new prince, and if there is the material that might afford one who is wise and ingenious the occasion to give it a form that would bring honor to him and good to all the people of Italy, it seems to me that so many things are concurring to favor a new prince that I know of no other time more appropriate than this. And if, as I have said,[1] it was necessary in order to see the capability of Moses that the people of Israel be slaves in Egypt, and to know the great courage of Cyrus that the Persians be oppressed by the Medes, and to know the excellence of Theseus that the Athenians be scattered; likewise, at the present time, in order to recognize the capability of an Italian spirit, it was necessary that Italy be reduced to the condition she is in at present, and that she be more of a slave than the Hebrews, more servile than the Persians, more scattered than the Athenians; without a leader, without order; beaten, despoiled, torn apart, overrun; and it was necessary for her to have put up with all kinds of desolation.

And even though before now some glimmer of light may have shown itself in the person of a certain man,[2] such that made it possible to believe that he was ordained by God for her redemption, nevertheless it was seen afterward how, at the culminating point of his career, he was rejected by fortune. So now she exists without life, she awaits that one who might heal her wounds and put an end to the sacking of Lombardy,[3] to the extortions in the Kingdom and in Tuscany, and cure those sores of hers which for so long a time have been festering. Look how she prays God that He may send someone to redeem her from these barbarous cruelties and outrages; look at her

al presente, in quale lei possa più sperare che nella illustre Casa Vostra, quale, con la sua fortuna e virtù, favorita da Dio e dalla Chiesa, della quale è ora principe, possa farsi capo di questa redenzione. Il che non fia molto difficile, se vi recherete innanzi le azioni e vita de' sopranominati. E benchè quelli uomini sieno rari e maravigliosi, nondimanco furono uomini; ed ebbe ciascuno di loro minore occasione che la presente; perchè la impresa loro non fu più iusta di questa, nè più facile, nè fu a loro Dio più amico che a voi. Qui è iustizia grande: « iustum enim est bellum quibus necessarium, et pia arma ubi nulla nisi in armis spes est ». Qui è disposizione grandissima; nè può essere, dove è grande disposizione, grande difficultà, pur che quella pigli delli ordini di coloro che io ho proposti per mira. Oltre di questo, qui si veggano estraordinarii, sanza esemplo, condotti da Dio: el mare si è aperto; una nube vi ha scorto el cammino; la pietra ha versato acqua; qui è piovuto la manna; ogni cosa è concorsa nella vostra grandezza. El rimanente dovete fare voi. Dio non vuole fare ogni cosa, per non ci torre el libero arbitrio e parte di quella gloria che tocca a noi.

E non è maraviglia se alcuno de' prenominati Italiani non ha possuto fare quello che si può sperare facci la illustre Casa Vostra, e se, in tante revoluzioni di Italia e in tanti maneggi di guerra, e' pare sempre che in quella la virtù militare sia spenta. Questo nasce che gli ordini antiqui di essa non erano buoni, e non ci è suto alcuno che abbi saputo trovare de' nuovi; e veruna cosa fa tanto onore a uno uomo che di nuovo surga, quanto fa le nuove legge e li nuovi ordini trovati da lui. Queste cose, quando

ever ready and willing to follow a banner, if only there were some person to raise it. There is no one in sight, at present, in whom she can have more hope than in your illustrious house,[4] that with its fortune and ingenuity, favored by God and by the Church,[5] of which it is now prince, could make itself head of this redemption. To do this would not be very difficult, if you keep before you the actions and lives of those named above.[6] And although those men are exceptional and phenomenal, they were nonetheless men, and each of them had less opportunity than the present; for their undertaking was not more just than this, nor simpler, nor was God more a friend to them than to you. There is much justice in this: "only those wars that are necessary are just, and those arms are holy without which there would be no hope."[7] There is a great willingness at present; and where there is great willingness there cannot be great difficulty, if you hold to the methods of those I have set up as targets.[8] Besides this, at present we have witnessed extraordinary happenings without precedent brought about by God: the sea has opened; a cloud has cleared your path; the rock has poured water; it has rained manna here; everything has run in favor of your greatness.[9] The rest you must do yourself. God does not want to do everything, so as not to take from us our free will and a part of that glory that belongs to us.

And it is no wonder if some of the Italians mentioned previously were not able to do what is hoped may be done by your illustrious house; and if, during the numerous revolutions in Italy and during the numerous manoeuvres of war, it always seems that her military strength is extinguished; this arises from the fact that her old methods were not good, and that there was no one who knew how to invent new ones; and nothing brings as much honor to a newly rising man as do the new laws

sono bene fondate e abbino in loro grandezza, lo fanno reverendo e mirabile. E in Italia non manca materia da introdurvi ogni forma: qui è virtù grande nelle membra, quando la non mancassi ne' capi. Specchiatevi ne' duelli e ne' congressi de' pochi, quanto gli Italiani sieno superiori con le forze, con la destrezza, con lo ingegno; ma come si viene alli eserciti, non compariscono. E tutto procede dalla debolezza de' capi; perchè quelli che sanno, non sono obediti; e a ciascuno pare di sapere, non ci sendo infino a qui alcuno che si sia saputo rilevare, e per virtù e per fortuna, che gli altri cedino. Di qui nasce che, in tanto tempo, in tante guerre fatte ne' passati venti anni, quando egli è stato uno esercito tutto italiano, sempre ha fatto mala pruova; di che è testimone prima el Taro, di poi Alessandria, Capua, Genova, Vailà, Bologna, Mestri.

Volendo, dunque, la illustre Casa Vostra seguitare quelli eccellenti uomini che redimerno le provincie loro, è necessario, innanzi a tutte le altre cose, come vero fondamento d' ogni impresa, provvedersi d' arme proprie; perchè non si può avere nè più fidi, nè più veri, nè migliori soldati. E benchè ciascuno di essi sia buono, tutti insieme diventeranno migliori, quando si vedranno comandare dal loro principe, e da quello onorare ed intrattenere. È necesario, pertanto, prepararsi a queste arme, per potere con la virtù italica defendersi dalli esterni. E benchè la fanteria svizzera e spagnola sia esistimata terribile, nondimanco in ambedua è difetto, per il quale uno ordine terzo potrebbe non solamente opporsi loro, ma confidare di superarli. Perchè li Spagnoli non possono sostenere e cavalli; e li Svizzeri hanno ad avere paura de'

and new methods invented by him.[10] These things, when they are well-established and carry with them the idea of greatness, will make him worthy of reverence and admiration.[11] And in Italy there is no lack of material to be given form; and at present there is great strength in her members, were it not for her lack of heads. Consider how in duels and clashes involving just a few the Italians are superior in force, dexterity and inventiveness; but when it comes to armies, they do not compare. And it all stems from the weakness of the heads; because those who know are not obeyed, and with everyone seeming to know, there has not been up to the present anyone who has known how to distinguish himself, by ingenuity and fortune, to the extent of making the others yield to him. As a result, during so much time, during the many wars waged over the past twenty years, whenever there was an entirely Italian army, it always made a bad showing. As proof of this there is first Taro,[12] then Alexandria,[13] Capua,[14] Genoa,[15] Vailà,[16] Bologna,[17] Mestri.[18]

Therefore, if your illustrious house wishes to follow those outstanding men who redeemed their lands, you should, above all other things, and as a true foundation for every enterprise, provide yourself with native troops; for you could not have more faithful nor more loyal nor better soldiers. And while each one of them alone is valiant, when all of them are united they will become even more valiant, having experienced the command of their prince and been honored and well treated by him. It is necessary, therefore, to provide yourself with troops such as these, so that with Italian strength you will be able to defend yourself from outsiders. And while the Swiss and Spanish infantries may be considered formidable, nevertheless both of them have defects so that a third army could not only oppose them but be confident of

fanti, quando li riscontrino nel combattere ostinati come loro; donde si è veduto, e vedrassi per esperienzia, li Spagnoli non potere sostenere una cavalleria franzese, e li Svizzeri essere rovinati da una fanteria spagnola. E benchè di questo ultimo non se ne sia visto intera esperienzia, tamen se ne è veduto uno saggio nella giornata di Ravenna, quando le fanterie spagnole si affrontorno con le battaglie todesche, le quali servono el medesimo ordine che le svizzere; dove li Spagnoli, con l' agilità del corpo e aiuti de' loro brocchieri, erono entrati, tra le picche loro, sotto, e stavano securi a offenderli sanza che li Todeschi vi avessino remedio; e se non fussi la cavalleria che li urtò, gli arebbano consumati tutti. Puossi adunque, conosciuto el difetto dell' una e dell' altra di queste fanterie, ordinarne una di nuovo, la quale resista a' cavalli e non abbia paura de' fanti: il che farà la generazione delle armi e la variazione delli ordini. E queste sono di quelle cose che, di nuovo ordinate, danno reputazione e grandezza a uno principe nuovo.

Non si debba, adunque, lasciare passare questa occasione, acciò che la Italia, dopo tanto tempo, vegga uno suo redentore. Nè posso esprimere con quale amore e' fussi ricevuto in tutte quelle provincie che hanno patito per queste illuvione esterne; con che sete di vendetta, con che ostinata fede, con che pietà, con che lacrime. Quali porte se li serrerebbano? quali populi li negherebbano la obedienzia? quale invidia se li opporrebbe? quale Italiano li negherebbe l' ossequio? A ognuno puzza questo barbaro dominio! Pigli, adunque, la illustre Casa Vostra questo assunto, con quello animo e con quella speranza che si pigliano le imprese iuste; acciò che, sotto la sua

overcoming them. For the Spanish cannot withstand men on horseback, and the Swiss will be frightened by foot soldiers they meet in battle who are as bold as themselves. So it has been seen and experience will show, the Spanish cannot withstand a French cavalry, and the Swiss are defeated by a Spanish infantry. And although this last case has not been entirely confirmed, nonetheless there was an indication of it at the battle of Ravenna,[19] when the Spanish infantry confronted the German battalions, which follow the same methods as the Swiss; and the Spanish, with their agile bodies and aided by their spiked shields, got under and through their pikes and into a position to attack them safely without the Germans being able to do a thing about it; and if it had not been for the cavalry that charged them, they would have killed all of them. Therefore, once the defects of both these kinds of troops are known, a new kind can be organized, which can resist horsemen and not be afraid of foot soldiers: this will be accomplished by creating new armies and changing battle formations. And these are among those things that, newly introduced, give prestige and greatness to a new prince.

This opportunity, then, must not be allowed to pass by, in order that Italy, after so long a time, may behold its redeemer. I cannot express with what love he will be greeted in all those provinces that have suffered through these foreign inundations; with what thirst for vengeance, with what firm loyalty, with what devotion, with what tears. What doors would be closed to him? what people would deny him obedience? what envy could oppose him? what Italian would not pay homage to him? This barbarian domination stinks to everyone! May then your illustrious house take up this mission with that courage and with that hope in which just enterprises are taken

insegna, e questa patria ne sia nobilitata e, sotto li sua auspizii, si verifichi quel detto del Petrarca:

> Virtù contro a furore
> Prenderà l' arme; e fia el combatter corto:
> Chè l' antico valore
> Nell' italici cor non è ancor morto.

NOTES

1. See Chapter vi.

2. A reference to Cesare Borgia (see Chapter vii).

3. After 1494 Lombardy was frequently invaded by the Swiss; in 1509 it fell to the French.

4. *The Prince,* it should be kept in mind, was dedicated to Lorenzo de' Medici, ruling Prince of Florence.

5. Cardinal Giovanni de' Medici became Pope Leo x in 1513.

6. Moses, Cyrus and Theseus, in particular, concerning whom Machiavelli says in Chapter vi ". . . from fortune they received nothing but the occasion, which in turn offered them the material they could then shape into whatever form they pleased; and without that occasion their very ingenuity would have been extinguished, and without that ingenuity the occasion would have come in vain."

7. An approximation of Livy ix, 1.

8. The image of the *target* recalls the opening paragraph of Chapter vi.

9. Biblical references from *Exodus* and *Numbers*.

10. See Chapters xii and xvii especially.

11. See Chapter xix.

up; so that, under your banner, this country may be en-
nobled and, under your auspices, those words of Petrarch
may come true:

> Ingenuity against rage
> Will take up arms and make the battle short.
> For the ancient valor
> In Italian hearts is not yet dead.[20]

12. On July 5, 1495, the French met the Italians in battle
at Fornovo (Parma) on the river Taro. Charles VIII led ten
thousand soldiers up from Naples and found his passage blocked
by an Italian army of forty thousand men under the command
of Gianfrancesco Gonzaga, Marquis of Mantua. Both armies
claimed victory, but the fact remains that the French passed
through Fornovo and continued their march northward.

13. Under Louis XII the French took the city in 1499.

14. In July 1501 a French army under Stuart d'Aubigny,
Cesare Borgia, and Francesco di San Severino plundered Capua.

15. Louis XII took Genoa in 1507.

16. See Chapters XII and XX. Julius II together with his allies
defeated the Venetians at Vailà in 1509.

17. Bologna was captured on May 21, 1511, by the French
under the command of G. J. Trivulzio.

18. In 1513 Mestri was burned by armies representing Spain
and the Papacy.

19. See Chapter XIII. Under the leadership of Gaston de
Foix the French were victorious at Ravenna on April 11, 1512.

20. From Petrarch's famous *canzone*, "Italia mia, benché il
parlar sia indarno" (lines 93–96).